LEADING
WITH EDGE

Activate Your Competitive Advantage Through Personal Insight

JOSE R. COSTA

Dedication

To Papá, Mamá, Cindy (the love of my life), Loren, Vera Rose, Nico, Gaby, Andy, Claudia, Jackie, Burt, and Juan Manuel: You're the "edge" in my life. Thank you for fueling my dreams, always supporting me, and for continuously reminding me that God is in control.

"For I know the plans I have for you," declares the Lord, "plans to prosper you and not to harm you, plans to give you hope and a future."
—Jeremiah 29:11

Contents

Introduction:
The Best Advice I Ever Got

I spent a lot of time at my father's office when I was a boy. Even when I was quite young, I knew that he was an example to follow: in our home, as a leader in our community, and as a great success in his business. I could tell by the way he carried himself and by the way others treated him. Even just walking in the front door of his office building gave me that sense. It was the kind of space that made an impression. The lobby was a big, open room with glossy white walls and high ceilings. On the right was an L-shaped couch where well-dressed people were often waiting to be called in for their meetings. Behind the couch there was an enormous poster that immediately called attention to itself, not just because of its size but because of its bright colors standing out against the monochromatic décor. It depicted a large school of blue fish going in one direction and one little orange fish trying to swim against them. Below the image was bold lettering that read, "Resist the Usual."

For me, that poster summed up everything my father taught me about how to succeed in business and make my way in the world: It was about having the courage to go my own way and do what was necessary to get there. That meant gaining as much knowledge and experience as I could, setting big goals and challenging myself, working hard to achieve what I wanted, and trusting that with

3

enough perseverance I would get where I wanted to go – even if everyone else was headed in the opposite direction.

My father was himself a kind of orange fish, always modeling this message for me and my three siblings. He was an immigrant from Spain. He came to Venezuela with his father, and in 1972 started a business from scratch. His first "office" was really just a rented house on the outskirts of the business district. By the mid-1990s he had moved into the gleaming offices that I remember so well and had built his company into a multimillion-dollar advertising agency, the largest of its kind in Venezuela. He partnered with the global agency Young & Rubicam ("Resist the Usual" was their slogan in the 1990s, and the poster had come from them) to create campaigns all over Latin America for multinational brands like Colgate, Citibank, Ford, and Diageo.

There is something about being that single orange fish in a sea of blue that gives a person real clarity about what he or she needs to do to succeed. My father reinforced that and other lessons throughout my entire childhood, but it wasn't until I left home and became an immigrant myself, moving to the United States to attend graduate school and then pursue my career, that I truly understood how valuable they were. What worked for my father also worked for me, giving me the *edge* I needed to propel myself forward in a competitive environment. The best advice my father ever gave me was to continue striving to gain that edge. He showed me how to have the daily courage and tenacity to pursue the things that would allow me to swim against the tide and stand out from the crowd.

***

If you're in business today and you're paying attention, then you have already read about the dismal employee engagement numbers that the Gallup organization posts year after year after year. The percentage of employees who are "not engaged" or "actively disengaged" has hovered around 70 percent for years, costing the U.S. economy trillions of dollars. How to get employees to perform better is a common topic among the leaders I've known. What often gets overlooked or ignored in the discussion, however, is the fact that Gallup cites "poor leadership" as one of the main causes of this continual and costly problem. W. Chan Kim and Renee Mauborgne, professors of strategy and management at INSEAD, wrote a *Harvard Business Review* article on this subject, "Blue Ocean Leadership," (May 2014) in which they noted: "Of course, managers don't intend to be poor leaders. The problem is that they lack a clear understanding of just what changes it would take to bring out the best in everyone and achieve high impact."

I currently serve as CEO of For Eyes, which is part of Grand-Vision, a global leader in optical retail with more than 7,000 stores worldwide, 120 of which are in the U.S. Before taking this position, I worked in a wide variety of industries — automotive, consumer products, quick-service restaurants, marketing and advertising, banking and private equity — and my personal experience backs up Gallup's conclusion. And I get it. As leaders, we have a lot on our minds — from keeping our customers happy and managing legal and compliance issues to keeping our eyes on the bottom line. How to truly engage and get the best out of people is not something we are typically taught in business school. Plus, if Gallup is right, then most of the leaders who came before us and have shown us the way really haven't excelled in this area either. Research shows that this is a longstanding problem across all industries.

What I have come to realize is that what it means to be a leader and what it truly takes to succeed as one are two things that far too often are in conflict with one another. It's time that we, as leaders, give the skill of leadership the same focus we would any other aspect of the job and teach others in our organization, the leaders coming up behind us, how to do the same. That is what I aim to do with this book. Its main goal is to help people resist the usual messages that are creating far too many poor leaders and take responsibility for the way they lead.

About This Book

This book is organized into four sections, each of which highlights a different key element that, if applied well and with consistency, can help anyone resist common leadership pitfalls and instead build a leadership style that gives them an edge. Based on my own experience, research, and the lessons of top leaders I have known (whose insights will also be included), these four elements are the keys to success:

1. Knowledge, and your ability to gain and share it;

2. Expectations, and your ability to model and drive them within an organization;

3. Hard work, especially when paired with big dreams;

4. Trust, in yourself and in the people around you.

Equally important is how you utilize these elements as a leader. I'm not the first person to talk about what makes someone an effective leader, but I often find that books and speakers on the subject don't talk much about the difficulty of applying these elements and making them relevant on a broad scale. Each of the elements I mentioned must be applied in a balanced way. That means they shouldn't be one-sided or driven by the leader alone. For example, you cannot apply a different set of expectations (Leading Edge #2) to those around you than you do to yourself — not if you want people to respect you and your position. On the flip side, you can trust people (Leading Edge #4) — in fact you must trust people if you want to get things done — but you have to do it with your eyes open and with a clear and honest view of their abilities and character.

I call this balanced application "the barbell approach." When I was in marketing at Burger King, we used something we called the barbell strategy to build our menus. Every menu needed value items on one end — those affordable, price-conscious items — that would drive traffic to our restaurants. At the same time, the menu needed premium offerings on the other end, items that would catch the customer's eye once they were in the restaurant and drive up the ticket. There was always something for the customers and something for us — a successful menu always needed an even balance of the two.

That is the same approach this book will take. For each of the four key elements, you will find two chapters: one that describes how to apply that element personally, in your own life and career, and another that shows how to promote it among the people around you. For example, Leading Edge #1 is about knowledge. The first chapter under that heading (Gaining Knowledge — Ask, Listen, and Be Curious) covers how you can gain more knowledge in order to give yourself an edge. The second chapter under that heading (Sharing Knowledge — Provide Feedback and Promote Know-How) addresses how to share knowledge and promote knowledge sharing in those around you, so that the whole team or organization has a deeper well to draw from in order to grow and succeed.

This barbell approach means there is something for you and something for your people in each of the elements being discussed. The balanced application of the right elements is what will allow you to continue to gain an edge time and time again. To help ensure you're on the right track, each section of the book ends with an assessment tool that will allow you to score yourself and monitor your progress.

When I talk about knowledge as one of the key elements for gaining an edge, I don't just mean knowledge about your business; I'm also talking about self-knowledge. My father served as a model for me, as someone who was continually learning and growing throughout his life, no matter how much success he had achieved. This is crucial because you can't gain an edge just once in your career. The world is ever changing and competition is never ending, so you always have to look for ways to expand your knowledge, skills, and experience. I was reminded of this recently when a mentor of mine gave me a piece of advice that I had heard over the course of my career but still hadn't been able to master. She said, "As a leader, you don't have to be liked; you have to be respected."

That really resonated with me. I spent much of my early career trying to win over the people around me. While there's nothing wrong with being liked, my mentor reminded me that it wasn't the thing that would make me a great leader; therefore, it wasn't where I should be focusing my energy. Her comments brought me back to that image of the fish from my father's office. The people who are most liked tend to be the ones swimming along with the group. Resisting the usual can be lot harder and a lot less popular, but I believe — as my father did — that doing so will help you gain the edge you need to achieve real results.

LEADING EDGE #1:
GAINING AND SHARING KNOWLEDGE

1: Gaining Knowledge—
Ask, Listen, and Be Curious

There are few who would deny the crucial role that knowledge plays in helping a person succeed in today's fast-paced, ever-changing business environment, but that doesn't mean that everyone knows how to go about gaining knowledge effectively and efficiently. After all, we are living in the Information Age where there is always another book or article you could read, podcast you could listen to, course you could take, and on and on. If you're not careful, you could spend all your time seeking knowledge, leaving little time for applying it.

In this chapter, I'm not going to talk about gaining knowledge for knowledge's sake, but the kind of strategic knowledge-seeking that leads to 1) better problem solving, 2) greater innovation, 3) stronger, more open relationships, and 4) less pressure on the leader to have all the answers. What's more, I'm going to talk about how you can gain knowledge without having to do all the work of seeking it out by yourself. In any group of people, knowledge has a flow. People can either guard what they know and keep their ideas to themselves, or they can share willingly, even eagerly, so that knowledge and ideas travel freely. The difference typically comes back to the leader and what sort of tone he or she has set. How can leaders set themselves up so that the right kind of knowledge is more likely to flow their way? That is what this chapter is all about.

Start With Humility

You may be wondering what humility has to do with gaining an edge through knowledge. Well, if you want knowledge to flow your way, you have to be willing to search for it. If you want people to share what they know with you, you have to be open to hearing it. Having humility as a leader means starting from a place of admitting you don't have all the answers and are not always going to make the right decisions.

That may sound simple, but it's one of those things that is easier said than done. No leader, parent, or person in a position of authority has all the answers but that can still be a hard thing for many to admit. If you are one of those leaders, then you are shutting yourself off from people who could have the information and insights you need.

When I was younger and working in marketing at a large quick-service restaurant chain, I worked under a Senior Vice President who thought she had all the right answers. When someone contradicted or challenged her, she would get into a screaming match with that person, and she wouldn't back down until he or she saw things her way — or pretended to. She wasn't interested in different viewpoints or getting to the best possible outcome. It was her opinion that mattered and getting her way was the only thing that satisfied her.

The result was a chaotic and fearful atmosphere in which people were reluctant to bring in new ideas, offer opinions, or even talk to her if they didn't have to. After all, most of us only have to be screamed at in front of our peers once before we think twice about putting ourselves in a situation like that again. I was no exception.

My team was working on a promotional campaign for our restaurants in Latin America, and this Senior Vice President had been clear about wanting us to focus our efforts on kids and families. At the same time, she never paid too much attention to our particular part of the business, so when our consumer insights took us in a different direction, we just followed where they were pointing. It was clear from our research that soccer was a big draw throughout the region, one that could provide us with some equally big marketing opportunities. At the same time, we discovered that our Spanish business unit had established a very successful partnership with the Spanish soccer league, La Liga. My team wanted to try something similar in the Latin American market. Our franchisees agreed that soccer was the right passion point to leverage, as did my direct boss who was president of the region.

When I discovered we could get the exclusive rights— for a very low dollar amount—to partner with the Spanish soccer league for our promotions, I made the deal. Furthermore, our beverage supplier agreed to put money toward the campaign. We got nearly 85 percent of Latin American countries where we did business to participate in the promotion. As part of the promotion, we offered crystal drinking glasses with soccer team logos on them to draw fans into our restaurants. We had purchased what we forecasted as about three months' worth of inventory of those glasses. They sold out in two weeks. It was the most successful campaign ever executed in our Latin American market. Everyone within the organization was thrilled with the results.

I was focused on the success of the business, and I had been able to get just about everyone else behind me. I had gotten the buy-in of all my team members, nearly all the franchisees who would be part of the promotion, and my direct boss, who was head of all regional business. We knew the Senior Vice President wasn't open to hearing what we had learned, so there was no use sharing our knowledge with her. When I one day found myself in a similar position of authority, I remembered that lesson and made a point of making sure people saw me as the kind of leader with whom they could exchange views (even if they differed with mine) and someone to whom they could comfortably bring controversial and potentially innovative ideas.

Keep Your Ego Out of the Way

A lack of humility can really cut you off from valuable knowledge and experience that others have to offer. It can also make it difficult for you to correct your course when you are headed down the wrong path. A lack of humility in leaders often shows up as a need to always be right. And no one is right all the time. Humble leaders who prioritize learning and getting to the best answers are more likely to catch themselves (or allow others to catch them) when they make a mistake. Those who can't admit when they're wrong, who can't put the right answer ahead of their need to be right, are more likely to dig their heels in and make a bad situation worse.

A friend of mine experienced this kind of situation when she was promoted to vice president of her division at a large food and beverage corporation. She had been promised that she could pick her own team, but when she got into her new role, the president, her direct boss, told her she had to find room for one particular person who had been with the company for years. Because of a restructuring, his position was being eliminated and they needed to find a place for him. My friend's team was that place, whether she liked it or not.

At first, because she was new to the organization, she didn't protest. She figured she could find a way to work with this person and that his institutional knowledge might come in handy. But it quickly became apparent that he was a serious problem. He was rude to his team members and often undermined my friend's authority in front of others. He was also way behind on his targets, but never took responsibility for it — it was always someone else's fault. To make matters worse, his overly familiar behavior had garnered some complaints from junior staff.

My friend kept bringing up these performance issues with her boss, but he wouldn't waiver. Finally, after several *years* of this kind of back and forth, he erupted at her, telling her never to mention the subject again. "I am tired of rehashing this subject," he said to her. "You just need to figure it out with him, and leave me out of it. Don't talk to me about it again." That was when she called me, looking for advice. "I can't just pretend this guy isn't a liability," she told me. "What am I supposed to do?"

It was a tough situation. "If I were you, I would stick to my guns... but carefully," I advised her. "If this employee continues to cause problems, I think it's your duty to make your boss aware of it, and probably others in the organization as well, if he's not listening. But don't push him too hard because that's not going to get you anywhere. And maybe it's time to start looking for opportunities elsewhere."

Not long ago I heard from my friend. After two years of this, her boss was finally getting ready to fire her terrible team member. The CEO had gotten wind of some of his failings and was forcing the president's hand. When her boss told her the news, he didn't say he was sorry for not listening to her sooner or admit that he had made a mistake. If he had, she might have respected him more and let it go. After all, we all have our blind spots (more on how to minimize those in chapter 3). As it stands, despite her stellar performance and that of her team over the past three years, she is quietly looking outside the company for new opportunities. She just feels that her boss's outsized ego makes it too difficult for her to do her best work. And she's right.

Practice Conspicuous Humility

It may sound counterintuitive, but humility is a quality that often needs to be put on display. If you believe you have all the answers, think you are always right, or are somehow above others because of your position, or if the people around you perceive that, then they aren't as likely to come to you with their knowledge, ideas, or opinions — not unless they have to.

So, how do you do this? There are acts of humility that you can make a point of practicing that will help people feel more comfortable around you, encourage them to be open and honest with you, and make it easier for them to contribute their thoughts and ideas. You can convey a sense of humility in big ways and small. Here are some simple ways that any leader can incorporate humility into his/her day-to-day work:

1) *De-emphasize hierarchy*: I never state my title when I introduce myself to someone, especially to someone junior to me. Saying I'm the CEO or in charge of such-and-such only reinforces a feeling of hierarchy or superiority. So does sitting in a big corner office while your team members crowd together in cubicles. That's why, when I became the CEO of For Eyes by GrandVision, I moved my desk, as well as those of all the company's managers, out to the floor so we could sit with our teams. In an article for *The Washington Post*, Paul Polman, CEO of Unilever, was once quoted as saying: "The moment you discover in life that it's not about yourself, that it is about investing in others, I think you're entering a steadier state to be a

great leader. Because above all, I think the main quality of a leader is to be a human being. There's no reason you are special because you happen to have this job." ("The Tao of Paul Polman" by Lillian Cunningham, *The Washington Post*, May 21, 2015.)

When I was in marketing at a quick-service restaurant chain, there was a franchise owner who was very successful. He owned close to one hundred restaurants in a region where the chain was very popular, and his business did very well. Over the years, he became a very wealthy guy and it showed. He drove an extremely expensive car. He dressed in extremely expensive, tailored suits. He always wore a big gold wristwatch. Everything about him screamed money and ostentatiousness. And this was how he would present himself when he walked into the fast food restaurants he owned — where the people working for him were only making about $7.00 an hour. Many of these people were barely making ends meet, so it was no wonder that his employees often seemed to lack energy or enthusiasm for their jobs. Based on what I saw, they were always polite to him, but I got the feeling that they didn't really like or respect him. He was successful, sure, but I always wondered how much *more* successful he could have been had he practiced humility in the way he presented himself to his team.

After meeting with this franchisee a few times, I became more conscious of how I dressed and presented myself around different people. I have nothing against you enjoying the fruits of your labor, but I do think that should be balanced against an awareness of and respect for other people's positions and circumstances. It's important for people to know who's in charge, but that's different from rubbing their faces in it.

2) *Put yourself in someone else's position*: In 2015, when I was president of Maaco, I had the unusual experience of being invited to participate in the CBS television show *Undercover Boss*. If you haven't

seen the show, the premise is to take senior executives from various companies and dress them up to go "undercover" in their own organizations. From there, they learn what it's really like to work on the front line. For me, that meant working in several different Maaco body shops around the country as a sander, painter, and detailer. Boy, was I humbled when I got my performance reviews from the bosses at those body shops. "Not fast enough," "too many mistakes," and "I wouldn't hire this guy on a permanent basis" were some of the things I heard at the end of my long workdays. It gave me a real appreciation for the hard work these guys do to please their customers and make their company a success.

Of course, most people won't get a chance to be on *Undercover Boss*, but that's okay. You can still get out of your office and spend a day in your warehouse, tour your stores, go on a sales call, or do whatever it is that applies to your particular business. Not only does this show employees that you are interested in their experience and expertise, it's also a good way find out what you don't know about how your business works. Chances are you will be surprised by how much you can learn.

3) *Give credit where credit is due*: I once had a boss who would take all the work that her team members had done and present it to her own boss under her name and her name alone. She never gave anyone credit, especially not in front of her superiors. It had such a negative impact on morale that it's amazing she never noticed.

The humble thing for her to have done would have been to be generous with her praise and credit. I'm not suggesting that you hand out credit just to make people feel good, but when someone has truly contributed something, it's an easy and effective motivational tactic to give that person credit for it. This is a simple way to ensure that people feel good about their good work and about you as a leader who notices and appreciates it. The best way to ensure that people want to contribute to your success is by helping them feel like it's shared success.

4) *Take an interest in people*: You never know what you can learn from someone, so it's important to keep the focus on others, not yourself. To make sure I do, I like to build it right into my schedule on a regular basis. I take people I work with—usually peer level or below, as well as vendors and clients—out for coffee or lunch as often as I can. I do that three to five times a week, every week without fail. I like to get people out of the office because I believe the change in setting helps them let their guard down and relax so they can open up. That has allowed for an enormous amount of good feedback and insight to come my way.

Recently I had to attend a golf event that the company was holding for its franchisees and vendors. My role that day was less about playing golf, but more about greeting franchisees and making guests feel valued and welcomed, which was probably a good thing since my golf game lacks serious game. I made the rounds before everyone started playing, but once they did, I had about four hours to kill before everyone came back to the clubhouse. I was just sitting there with some junior-level employees who were helping to run the event, so I asked an entry-level guy if he wanted to ride around in a golf cart with me to check on our franchisees. I used those thirty minutes we were riding together to get to know him and ask him questions. During the course of our conversation, he mentioned that he would like to try working in operations rather than marketing. It just so happened that I had a position in operations that needed to be filled. Because I took the opportunity and listened with an open mind, I had already found a great candidate before I had even formally started looking to fill the position.

Ask Good Questions

When you sit down with somebody for lunch or a ride in a golf cart, how do you get the right kind of information out of that person? How do you steer the conversation toward subjects that will be useful while making the person want to open up and share their knowledge with you? In other words, what makes a good question?

If it's someone I have never met before or don't know very well, I usually start with the personal: "Where did you grow up?" "How many brothers and sisters do you have?" "Where did you go to school?" "What did your parents do?" Questions like these are meant to be easy to answer, so the person feels comfortable talking to you right away. They are also meant to show your interest in them so they are more willing to open up.

Next, I often shift to questions that will tell me something about how curious the person is. I ask things like: "What books have you read?" "What do you do with your free time?" Curious people are interested in expanding their knowledge, and those are the kinds of people I like to surround myself with.

Then, I move on to the person's current function and get them talking about what they do, what they are working on, and what gets them excited. From there, I always ask this question: "In three to five years, where do you want to be?" I want to know if they want my job, if they want to be the head of finance, if they are simply happy where they are, or something else. Based on the answer, I then present a business challenge.

That is what I did with the young man with whom I shared the golf cart at our franchisee event. His name was Scott, and based on what he told me about himself, I asked him what he would do if he were suddenly given a position in operations like he wanted. Scott told me that he liked working with franchisees, and the first thing he would do would be to reach out to them to establish relationships. He said, "I would fly out to meet as many of them as I could and just start a conversation with them about what their issues are, how much money they're making, how they think they can make more money, and so on. Then I would follow up with calls to keep the conversation going. Obviously I can't be visiting all our franchisees every month, but I would try to go back as often as I could."

Scott was in his late twenties and didn't have a lot of experience per se, but the way he answered the question showed me something about how he thinks, how he approaches problems, and how he would handle a new situation. It was enough to make me want him on my team.

Learn How to Listen

When it comes to gaining the knowledge you need to get ahead, it should be obvious that it's important to know how to listen. But you might be surprised at the number of leaders I have met over the years, even ones who have climbed pretty high up the corporate ladder, who have not mastered this basic skill. And it shows.

Whenever I promote someone, my first piece of advice is to start off by getting to know the people who work there: ask them questions and then just listen with an open mind to what they have to say. I did this on a large scale during my first days as president of Maaco. I had come from the restaurant business, having worked for Burger King and KFC, so it wasn't surprising that there were those in my new company who doubted whether I could do the job, particularly some franchisees who wondered pretty publicly, "What does this burger guy know about cars?" That was why I spent my first ninety days at Maaco on what I called my *listening tour*. Instead of launching new initiatives or trying to prove myself, I traveled the country, visited all our body shops, and asked questions. And I didn't just ask questions;

I listened closely to the answers.

When I showed up for these visits and meetings, I made a point of taking a humble approach. I didn't show up with a team of twenty people. The first couple weeks it was me and the head of operations, and then it was just me. I would show up in a basic rental car, nothing fancy, dressed in a Maaco shirt and khakis. I always brought doughnuts for the crew and started off with a tour of the body shop. I met everyone and handed out the doughnuts. Then I

> **Elements of an Effective Conversation**
>
> 1. Start with the personal
>
> 2. Find out how curious the person is
>
> 3. Ask about the details of the person's current job
>
> 4. Ask where the person sees himself/herself in the future
>
> 5. Present the person with a hypothetical challenge to talk through

would end up in the owner's office, where I'd spend a couple of hours just asking questions: "What has your relationship with Maaco been like?" "What sort of relationship did you have with the company's founder, Tony Martino?" "What are your thoughts on how the brand has evolved?" "What are your biggest challenges?" I would then take out my notebook and record the owner's insights, observations, and anything else I wanted to follow up on. Doing so ensured that the owner knew I had heard him.

Sometimes I had to listen to some tough feedback. When I first showed up, many franchisees were very opinionated, saying that I didn't have enough experience or the right qualifications. One guy even told me: "You're too young and you're not American. This is an American company, and that matters." It was harsh stuff, but I didn't let my ego get in the way. I just nodded and let him vent. I was the president; I couldn't just walk away. Well, I guess I could have, but that wouldn't have been very useful. It never helps to bury your head in the sand just because things get tough. After all, you can't solve a problem you can't see.

Because I hung in there, the experience paid off in many ways: I knew where people stood ideologically and what they were really thinking. I gained insight into how the business had evolved, how it was working at that time, and what the issues were. It was also helpful for the franchisees to get to know me and see that I cared about what they had to say. It gave me a chance to tell them, "I hear you. I understand your concerns. Give me a chance to show you how we're going to change this together. And if we don't, then I want you to tell me what I'm doing wrong."

For a lot of these franchisees, I think the conversations were mostly about airing their frustrations. They had seen too many guys come in with big promises that they didn't always deliver on. Because I listened and respected what they had to say instead of making big promises right off the bat, they respected me more. When I came back to them a few months later with a new vision for the business that I wanted to roll out, they were willing to hear me out because I had heard them out. I quickly got the endorsement of the franchisee council — the top fifteen franchisees in the system — for that new vision, which made it a whole lot easier to get support from the rest of the system. And when I left the company, we had had sixty months of consecutive same-center sales growth. So we were doing something right. Just before I moved on, I was still visiting franchisees on a regular basis, and by then they received me with open arms.

Listen So Others Feel Heard

It's important to know how to listen in order to gain knowledge, certainly, but it's also a crucial skill to build better relationships with the people we work with. When someone feels heard, it fosters a sense of trust and respect between you. And when people trust and respect you, they are more likely to share with you what they think and what they know. They are more likely to listen to you when you talk or present them with new ideas. They are more likely to give you the benefit of the doubt.

This means that you need to know how to listen and how to listen in a way that lets people know you hear them and respect what they have to say. Here are some key ways to make sure that happens:

1) *Maintain strong eye contact*: For me, this is the most important thing. We have all had the experience of talking with someone who is looking past us or whose eyes are darting about as we talk. The person may be listening, they may not, but the point is, how can we know for sure?

2) *Actively listen*: You can do this by periodically repeating back your understanding of what the other person has said for confirmation or by asking questions when you need clarification. People are much more likely to feel heard if you participate actively in the conversation rather than just sit passively and listen.

3) *Minimize distractions*: We are living in a time when we carry distractions around with us in our pockets, and far too often people try to multitask when they should be focusing. No one is going to feel heard or respected if you are on your phone or computer throughout a meeting. So don't take out your phone. Recent research has shown that the mere presence of your phone—even if you aren't using it—

reduces the quality of conversation between people. Leave your phone in your pocket or turn it facedown on the table with the volume off. Whomever you're talking to will know you're paying attention to them, not your phone.

4) *If appropriate, take notes*: This shows the person that you are invested in what they have to say. It's also a very useful habit to get into so you aren't missing or forgetting important information. Related to the point above, I try to do this with a pen and notebook as much as possible rather than on my laptop. In order to minimize distractions, I only bring my laptop to meetings if I need to see a presentation or be online for some reason.

These tips aren't hard to apply, but you do need to make a point of practicing them on a regular basis. You might be surprised by how much of a difference it makes to really know how to make people feel heard. By the end of my listening tour at Maaco, I had a much deeper understanding of this new business I was in, and I had begun to build solid relationships with many of the franchisees who had originally been wary of me. That is one of the biggest benefits of seeking out knowledge in the right way from those around you. Even if the people you are listening to tell you things you have heard before or things you disagree with, hearing them out makes them feel valued, and it builds trust, which you are going to need if you want them on your side in order to accomplish big things, together, down the line.

Be an Avid Learner

When you start from a place of knowing that you don't have all the answers and that you're not right all the time, no matter how much experience you have or how high you have risen in the ranks, it allows you to approach things from a different perspective. To grow instead of stagnate, one of the best things anyone can do is adopt an attitude of curiosity. This means being an avid learner who actively seeks out knowledge, not just among your team members but throughout your organization, industry, and beyond. Here are some of the different ways you can become an active learner no matter what your role:

1) *Expand your network*: Scheduling the kind of regular lunches or meetings that I mentioned earlier in this chapter is a great place to start. Reach out beyond your immediate circle to connect with people at different levels, in different departments, with different skills.

2) *Read!* I read every morning for about an hour. By making this a regular habit, I get through one or two books every week. I also keep up with about twelve different news and industry websites including *Harvard Business Review*, *Advertising Age*, *Fast Company*, *The Wall Street Journal*, *The New York Times*, *Forbes*, *Institutional Investor*, and *Bloomberg*. Early in my career, I was very focused on marketing and business, so most of my reading focused on those topics. Since then, I have realized that I can optimize my capacity for new ideas, insights, and self-reflection by casting a wider net. I read a daily scripture from the Bible, and in any given month, my nightstand may hold books on sociology, psychology, biography, and more.

3) *Continue your education*: I have three master's degrees because I believe so strongly in education, and I would go back to school for a fourth one if I had the time. But even if you can't invest in a formal degree program, that doesn't mean you can't keep learning in a less formalized way. I sign up for a week-long executive class about once a year to expand my skills in things like negotiations (at Harvard Business School's Executive Education program), mergers and acqui-

sitions (at the University of Chicago), innovation (at Northwestern's Kellogg's School of Management) and leadership (at the Center for Creative Leadership). I also go to a monthly breakfast at my church, where we learn about different topics that aren't strictly business-related, but I almost always find some lesson that I can apply. For example, at one of these breakfasts, a high school football referee was asked to give a speech about what he does and the different challenges he faces. He talked about how he handles it when a coach is so mad about a call that he runs on the field and gets in the referee's face. It happens often enough, even in high school sports, that this guy had developed a specific way of dealing with it. As the coach runs toward him, he maneuvers himself slowly so that his back is to the audience. That way the entire stadium of people can see that coach as he screams and carries on. It puts his behavior on display and often makes him feel intimidated when he realizes he's being watched. It causes most people to calm down and moderate their behavior without the referee having to say a thing. I love this strategy and believe it could be applied in all sorts of situations, anytime you find yourself involved in a public confrontation where emotions are running high.

4) *Get involved with different organizations*: I recently joined YPO (Young Presidents' Organization), which is like a networking and learning group for executives and entrepreneurs. It's a great way to learn about the kinds of challenges other people face in different situations and industries and how leaders go about tackling those challenges. There are all kinds of professional organizations out there that you can join if you take time to identify them. The key is to take advantage of the knowledge these organizations connect you too. For example, during our YPO meetings, I ask basic questions that help me understand the leader in context to the success of his business. "What has made you so successful?" "What's the best new idea you've

encountered lately?" "How do you communicate what's important to your team?"

My YPO group once visited a manufacturing company in Greensboro, North Carolina, to learn more about its operations. As we were walking through the plant, I saw this vending machine filled with bolts, screws, and nails. I couldn't help myself: "What's that?" I asked. The executive who was giving us the tour told us about a company that offered this product line of vending machines for industrial customers, which helped prevent theft and waste. The way it worked was that you gave employees their own card to use to get whatever supplies they needed. What they took was recorded in their account. If they need X amount of screws, for example, that is exactly how many screws the machine would give them. I thought it was a brilliant idea, one that I filed away for potential use in the future.

5) *Constantly be on the lookout for new learning opportunities*: More than any individual tactic, the important thing about being an avid learner is to adopt it as a mind-set. Opportunities are everywhere if you just look. Recently I joined the board of a science and technology museum for kids in my hometown of Charlotte, North Carolina. The board was looking for someone with my expertise, and I figured it would be a great way to give back to the local community while also learning about new subject areas—for me and for my three small children.

Learn About Yourself

If you want to grow, improve, excel, and become better at what you do each and every day, you need to take an active part in learning about yourself—your strengths, your opportunities for improvement, how you come across to others, and so on. Don't wait for an annual performance review from your boss. Ask your boss how you're doing if he or she isn't letting you know on a regular basis. And don't stop there. Ask your peers and your direct reports what they think. Then go outside the organization and get different perspectives on your work and your leadership abilities whenever and wherever you can.

How can you do this? Start by simply asking. And then keep asking until you get the information you need. For example, early in my career I had a boss who never seemed invested in his employees. I wasn't sure if he thought I was doing a good job, so in addition to our quarterly review sessions, I asked if we could have a monthly development meeting where he would coach me. I wanted to be in his position one day, so I figured who better to learn from than him?

We set up a regular appointment, but he missed the first one. He made it to the one after that, but it was always hit or miss whether he was going to show. I finally got frustrated enough that I took a different approach.

The person who had previously held my boss's position had gone on to start his own company. I knew him a little bit because we still worked with his company on occasion as a vendor. One day I called him and asked if I could take him to lunch. We talked about the business for a bit, and once we had established a rapport, I asked if he could tell me what it had been like to be in my boss's position when he worked for the company and what skills he thought I would need to fill it myself one day.

He was very open with me and gave me a lot of great advice. We kept in touch after that, and eventually I asked him if he would be a mentor to me on a more formal basis by meeting regularly to help me develop as a leader. He agreed and became an invaluable resource. Even though he didn't work with me on a day-to-day basis, he got to know enough about me to really help me become the kind of leader who could grow into bigger and bigger roles.

Learning about yourself really comes back to humility. You have to be willing to ask the tough questions about yourself and let people give you the tough answers. You have to be willing to see yourself clearly because if you don't, you will never be able to grow past your current limitations.

Never Go It Alone

We started this chapter talking about leaders who don't like to admit when they're wrong or don't have all the answers. One final, crucial but rarely discussed reason why these are counterproductive attitudes is because they isolate the leader even more than is necessary. It can be lonely to be the leader, but if you adopt an attitude of curiosity about people and things, if you make a point of getting to know people at all levels, asking them questions and listening so they feel heard, being the leader can suddenly become a lot less lonely.

Leaders have to know how to shoulder responsibility — there is no way around that. But they also need to know how to manage the pressures that come with the job. It takes some of the pressure off if you are willing to collaborate with others, to share credit, to find out what others know that you don't. It can be empowering to feel like you are in this together, but you will never get there without humility, trust, and respect for those around you, for all they know, and for all they have to contribute. You don't have to be all on your own in making big decisions. Ultimately, accountability lies with you, but the concepts and tactics we have talked about in this chapter can help. They can help a lot.

2: Sharing Knowledge—Provide Feedback and Promote Know-How

In the last chapter, I started off by talking about humility and how leaders need it in order to adopt an attitude of curiosity that allows them to learn and grow. The same is true for everyone, not just the leader, and if leaders can encourage this same attitude in those around them, then the edge that knowledge can give will only be compounded. More people will be better positioned to solve problems, innovate, and build better relationships, which can only be good for the organization as a whole.

In my view, there are two main things that make a person great: the absorption and application of insightful feedback from others and depth of experience (think Malcolm Gladwell's 10,000 Hour Rule). These are the two things that, when cultivated on a regular basis, help people to continually expand their knowledge and capabilities.

Providing feedback is one of the most crucial tools leaders can use to spread knowledge, which is why it's so important that they learn how to do it well. All too often, performance reviews (the most common type of feedback in most companies) are just boxes leaders check off on their to-do lists. They aren't used to offer the kind of feedback people need to really improve. Of course, feedback is just one tool leaders have at their disposal to help spread knowledge. In this chapter, I will also talk about other ways to bring more knowledge to more people within your organization—encouraging knowledge sharing and by setting challenges for people so they are constantly developing their skills and expanding their experiences.

The Art of Feedback

I don't think anyone truly likes to be humbled, even though it's important for all of us to know how to keep our egos in check. A healthy sized ego is required if someone wants to position himself/ herself to continually learn and grow. That's why it's so important that leaders go about encouraging humility in ways that lead to better results—not turning people off, pushing them away, or deflating their sense of self. The way to promote humility in the people around you is, first and foremost, by providing honest and directed feedback that's aimed at helping them expand their knowledge about them- selves and their work, to grow personally and professionally. You can help someone become great by being their mirror, by helping them see clearly what they are good at, what they are not so good at, and how they are succeeding overall, not just in terms of the organiza- tion's goals, but in terms of their personal goals as well.

This is such an important tool that I'm going to spend quite a lot of time on it in the coming pages. I have seen so many leaders do this badly, or simply ineffectively. I will talk about the most powerful ways to deliver the kind of feedback that makes a difference. I will also talk through the different kinds of feedback that leaders can use as tools, including formal feedback, regular or less formal feedback, and spontaneous feedback.

Formal Feedback

Quarterly or annual performance reviews are the norm in most organizations. I'm going to show some examples from the format I use in order to take you through the process. You may want to use some version of this format, or you may have your own format that you use to provide feedback — either way is fine. One of the main things you want to do is to be as consistent about the format as possible. Once you find a format that works for you, stick with it so that people can compare their current reviews to their past ones to get a picture of the progress they are making over time.

I believe strongly in the principle of *simple and focused*. That's why every performance review I do for every employee fits on one page. As you can see in the example here, the one-pager covers three key areas: 1) strengths, 2) opportunities, and 3) a matrix on which I plot the person's standing in the company *at the time of the review*.

When it comes to a person's strengths and opportunities, again I believe in simple and focused. That's why I highlight just three to five points in each category. That means that during our in-person review, we will have time to talk through the three to five things that the team member is doing really well and the three to five ways in which he or she could improve. The latter includes things they can work on to improve the business *and* things they can work on to improve themselves, because if a team member becomes more effective as a person, then the business becomes more effective. This combination is key (more on this in the coming pages).

The other element is a matrix that shows at a glance where someone stands within the organization. The two main things that I consider when plotting someone on this graph are *Performance*, which is the horizontal axis, and *Potential*, which is the vertical axis. Performance is about whether that person is delivering results. Potential is about whether that person can rise within the organization.

Everyone will fit within one of the boxes on this graph. Someone who is new to the organization or has recently moved to a new role is likely to have a lot of potential but not much of a track record just yet in terms of performance. That person would likely fall within the top left box — High Potential/Low Performance. Someone who is meeting their objectives but not exceeding expectations would be in the middle box — Medium Potential/Effective Performance. Someone who is a star and has just been knocking it out of the park in terms of growth and performance would be in the top right box — High Potential/High Performance. Those are the best people within your organization.

Someone who has been performing very well, but who isn't really growing or expanding would be in the bottom right box — Low Potential/High Performance. This isn't necessarily a bad place to be for everyone. Some people — those in a technical position perhaps, like forensic accounting or engineering — will master a skill and then continue working at it for the rest of their lives. These are the pillars of your organization, the people you can rely on to perform, quarter after quarter, but who may not have aspirations to rise any higher. That's fine for some people, as long as they're comfortable in that box and don't feel like they're being held back. Pointing out this category during the review gives you a change to gauge whether the employee is happy in that category or not — and then you can coach accordingly.

Finally, in the bottom left box are those who have Low Potential/Low Performance. This is the problem area. If someone spends two performance reviews in the bottom left box, then it's time to have a conversation about exiting the company because that person isn't making a big enough contribution to the organization. Providing formal feedback in this way gives people an opportunity to improve, but if you end up having to let them go, they can't say that you didn't warn them, which is equally important.

Where someone falls on this graph shows them, at a glance, how valuable they are to the organization and whether they are in danger of losing their position. The important thing is to make this as clear as possible. It's not uncommon for team members to be with a company for a while and feel they should be promoted. When they don't get those opportunities, or when they see someone getting them when they aren't, it breeds bad feelings and diminishes motivation. If you are evaluating someone every quarter, then it should come as no surprise when someone is passed over. All people have to do is look back at their recent performance reviews to understand why they aren't moving up the ranks.

Simple. Focused. Easy to understand at a glance. All contained on one page. This is what I aim for. I don't want anyone to ever walk away from a performance review confused or feeling overwhelmed by too much information. Of course, this one-pager is just the start. It's what opens a conversation between you and your team member, one that will help you better understand each other and get on the same page in terms of expectations. Now, let's talk through some of the different ways that ensuing conversation can go and how you can effectively steer it to get the results you want—the kind that will give you and your organization that edge you are looking for.

Q1 Performance Review
Employee A

Strengths:

1. Customer relations

2. Collections process

3. Execution of new programs

Opportunities:

1. Market planning and development

2. Retail traffic decline

3. Quality and frequency of communications to team

	Low Performance	Effective Performance	High Performance
High Potential	Employee A Q1 Performance		
Medium Potential			
Low Potential			

Hard-to-Hear Feedback

Oftentimes the feedback you need to deliver during performance reviews won't be easy for the team member to hear. That doesn't mean you shouldn't be honest or direct about it. But it does means that you need to be conscious of how the person is receiving your feedback and look for ways to coach him or her through it in a constructive way. This last part is often overlooked, which is too bad because what good is honest, direct feedback if the person receiving it isn't able to internalize it?

The review for Employee A is a good example. This team member had performed well in the past, which showed me that he had potential, but his performance during this particular quarter wasn't very good, which was why I put him in the High Potential/Low Performance box in the bottom graph. When you are doing a performance review, you want to make sure people understand that you aren't judging their overall value to the company since they arrived. You aren't judging their value as a person. You are simply reviewing their performance over a specific period of time, in this case a single quarter.

Making this clear can help a person be more receptive to tough feedback. After all, everyone has some ups and downs over the course of their career. Still, Employee A got defensive as we talked through his one-pager. He tried to defend the retail traffic decline, for example, which I had listed as an opportunity. When I asked him to back up what he was saying, he gave me examples from previous quarters. I assured him he was right; he had done well in this area during those times, but we were now talking about the past quarter, a period when he hadn't shown the same results. This is why it's so important to talk these things through and invite people to disagree rather than just hand them their report card. It's through these kinds of conversations that you find clarity. When I framed things this way for Employee A, his defenses came down. He wasn't happy about the feedback, but he understood what I meant.

My one-pagers are designed to help people take a hard look at themselves. I will talk more in the coming sections about how to set up these kinds of conversations so both sides can get something out of them that can be used moving forward. The main thing to understand right now is that if you really want to be effective, you have to make it your job to help people digest difficult feedback and use it to propel themselves forward. Simply relaying the information isn't enough.

Q1 Performance Review
Employee B

Strengths:

1. Supply chain results

2. Project management and execution

3. Market integration

Opportunities:

1. Better process around market planning

2. Short-term plan on how to implement CRM program

3. Deeper networking and collaboration with other team members

	Low Performance	Effective Performance	High Performance
High Potential			Employee B Q1 Performance
Medium Potential			
Low Potential			

Easy-to-Hear Feedback

In contrast, we have the review for Employee B, who is really an all-around star performer. Of course, when you have a team member like this one, it makes the performance review easy, even a pleasure. That doesn't mean, however, that our conversation was just a love fest. In fact, some of your best opportunities for growth come from those in your organization who are already great at growing the business. When someone is doing excellent work, it's the perfect time to talk about how that team member can keep the momentum going, expand on his/her success, and rise even higher.

During my review with Employee B, I spent time praising his successes in order to reinforce the good behaviors that got him there. And even though I didn't have any major criticisms for him, I still made a point of covering small things, tweaks he could do here or there, in order to grow his department even more and move to a position of greater authority in the future. I suggested he improve some of his processes around market planning and implement a customer relations management program that would help him find additional growth opportunities.

I also focused on this star performer's personal and leadership skills. I see in him the potential to grow into positions with more responsibility, something that he's eager to do. But in order to do that, he needs to broaden his contacts within the company, reach beyond those he deals with on a regular basis. I suggested he work on net-working with people outside his department so that when it comes time for a promotion, there will be more people (besides me) who know him and are willing to support him. That is something tangible he can start doing right away for the sake of the company *and* for the sake of his own career.

Steps for Making Performance Reviews Count

As leaders, we don't want to give people feedback just on how they're doing. We want to give people feedback in ways that create change. We want people to walk away from a performance review with the knowledge and perspective they need to make a difference over the next month, quarter, or year. The following steps will help you steer the conversation in a more productive, more empowering way so you can deliver the kind of feedback that counts:

1) *Set the right context*: I always send my one-page review summaries to employees in advance of our performance review meetings so they can read them and give them some thought beforehand. I also do it so no one is taken by surprise or feels ambushed in the meeting room. This gives people a chance to prepare themselves for what's coming, which is especially important if there is a difficult conversation ahead.

Then, when employees show up for their performance review, I like to sit next to them, rather than across from them, with the one-pager in front of us. When you sit across the table from someone, there's a barrier between you, and it feels more confrontational. I like to try to make people feel like we are on the same side; sitting next to them helps to foster that feeling in a subtle way.

2) *Start with the opportunities*: I start the conversation by talking about the person's opportunities, and then I move on to their strengths. I do this for the simple reason that it allows me to get the tough stuff out of the way first, and then we can end the meeting on a more positive note.

3) *Keep it simple and focused*: I always fit the review on one page, highlighting no more than three to five things in the two key categor-

ies: opportunities and strengths. That is plenty for a person to focus on over the course of a single quarter. More than that is just too much. If you really want to help someone grow, you have to help that person stay focused on the key things. It's far too easy in today's business world, with all the information that comes at us, to have divided attention in which a person may never make significant progress in any one area of work.

4) *Be objective and offer proof*: It's important that you don't allow your feedback to come across as overly subjective, as simply your opinion or point of view. If you do, it will carry less weight and often make people feel it's about whether or not you like them rather than how they are performing for the company. That's why I always prepare when I create my one-pager and make sure I come into performance review meetings with information to back up each and every one of the points I have made — opportunities and strengths. I take an objective position as I go through each point, give examples, offer other people's point of view, and mention any relevant figures like sales numbers or customer feedback scores.

Using tangible examples of things that have happened recently is often the most effective way drive a point home. Let's say someone did a very good job of presenting a financial analysis during a recent meeting. If I'm praising that person's analytical skills as a key strength, then I will take him back to that presentation and remind him what was so effective about it. This helps make the feedback more concrete and digestible for people.

5) *Make it personal (in the right way)*: Too many leaders neglect this point. You don't want people to feel personally attacked. At the same time, feedback is so much more effective when it helps someone grow as a person and as a leader, when it's about skills and attributes they can use anywhere, not just in their specific role in this specific com-

pany. By this I mean things like their leadership skills, communication skills, networking abilities, strategic thinking, etc. Of course, you need a balance. You want to talk about business results *and* about their personal qualities. It's the latter, however, that I believe too many leaders forget to focus on.

I once had a boss who never wanted to talk about me as a person. It was always 100 percent business. It really bothered me because selfishly, if it's a performance review, I want feedback about me—not just about the metrics in my department. For one thing, I already knew what the numbers were. What I didn't know was what my boss thought about me and how much growth potential I was showing.

Looking back to the review for Employee A, I pointed out that he is too hands-off in terms of market planning and development and that he communicates too infrequently with his team members. He leaves things up to his team members without doing enough to monitor their progress. That doesn't mean his team members don't do a good job. If people are getting the job done well, then great; I'm all for staying out of their way. But a leader needs to consistently monitor progress so he can step in when there's a problem or facilitate things to get done in a faster, better way if possible. When something goes wrong, Employee A had a tendency to blame his team rather than take responsibility. That's a leadership skill that he could work on, which will benefit him wherever he is.

6) *Allow them to react*: Once we have talked through all the elements on someone's one-page review, I always pause for a moment to let him or her take everything in. Then I give them a chance to react. As leaders, we aren't always right, so when processing feedback, people should be encouraged to respond and give their point of view about what we have said. Of course, if we have done our homework and can support each of the points we have gone over, then employees aren't likely to talk us out of our viewpoint. But they may still

have something to say that's useful. In addition, hearing people out conveys empathy and respect, making it more likely that they will walk away willing to seriously consider what you have said, even if it has been critical.

When I give people a chance to react, typically one of three things happens: 1) they accept everything I have said without protest (this is particularly likely with those who have received positive reviews), 2) they restate back to you, in their own words, what you have told them in an effort to understand and process the feedback or to show you that they have been listening, or 3) they protest certain things that you have said. Any of these three responses are valid. In fact, the second and third responses help to further the conversation and promote clarity. Sometimes people need to talk things through in order to really understand and internalize the feedback.

If people want to give me some coaching or feedback in return, I welcome that too. Employee A did that in a recent performance review after he had gotten some pretty tough feedback from me. I love competition, so at a recent meeting, I had compared his performance to that of another employee in the department, someone who had been getting top-notch results. I said that "unfortunately" Employee A had not gotten the same level of results. What I said was true, and my comparison didn't mean that Employee A was doing a bad job. It just meant that he wasn't doing as well as someone else, and I had hoped the sense of competition might spur him on. Employee A brought that up during our review and told me that he didn't appreciate it. If I had problems with his performance, he would prefer if I talked to him one-on-one rather than embarrassing him in front of his peers. It was a fair point, so I accepted it and thanked him for telling me. It was a good moment, one that helped us establish a stronger, more candid relationship and showed Employee A how a leader can take tough feedback as a positive—a chance to be more aware and do better in the future—rather than a negative.

7) *End with a question*: At the end of every performance review, I always wrap things up with a question: "Did anything that I presented to you today catch you by surprise?" Because I use the same format for performance reviews every quarter, people can look back and see for themselves if they have made progress or not. I also have regular contact with my direct reports throughout the quarter (more on this in the next sections), so they should never be caught by surprise. That's your goal. It's such an important goal that you want to make sure you are doing it right. The way in which people answer that question will provide you with a measure of how you're doing as a leader in terms of keeping them informed, on task, and growing in the right direction.

Regular, Less Formal Feedback

Related to that last point, you don't want people to be surprised when they find out that they aren't doing very well. If someone is failing, or even just falling behind, it's important to communicate that early and often. It's equally important to communicate when someone is doing well to help the person stay motivated and on track. To ensure these things, it's important that feedback isn't confined to your quarterly or annual review process. All too often, leaders get busy and don't keep up the kind of regular contact with team members that ensures success.

Not all feedback requires a one-page or written report. Most of the time, what's in order is simple contact and conversation. Regular meetings with key team members between formal performance reviews should be a priority for any leader. One of the best ways to ensure they happen is to make a habit of them. I have built into my schedule weekly one-on-ones with each team member, monthly forecast meetings, monthly financial meetings, and monthly business review meetings. In our weekly one-on-ones, I try to be thorough so I'm never caught by surprise when something isn't getting done. We discuss every one of the person's direct reports and every one of their top projects and priorities. I also ask a lot of questions: I ask for updates. I ask if they have encountered any obstacles. I ask how I can help them move things forward more quickly. This is how I ensure that I stay on top of things and that I'm always providing continuous feedback.

Spontaneous Feedback

It's also crucially important to look for opportunities to give feedback spontaneously because that's often the most effective kind. When something has just happened and is fresh in a person's mind, the feedback tends to have more power.

To give an example, I was once watching one of my department heads give a presentation during our annual convention. He was on stage in front of thousands of people in a big auditorium and that understandably made him a bit nervous. The problem was that it showed up in an odd quirk. As he was making a very persuasive presentation, his presence was undercut by the fact that he was standing up there swaying back and forth. He looked a little bit like a see-saw and it was highly distracting.

When my department head came off stage, I pulled him aside and told him what a wonderful job he had done. I wasn't blowing smoke. By and large, he had given a great presentation. I told him: "You were eloquent. You moved your hands well. You engaged the audience. I have just one small piece of coaching that I want to give you to help make you even better next time. If you plant your feet squarely and stand with your legs parallel to your shoulders as you face the audience, it will convey more confidence."

He immediately understood what I was talking about. He thanked me and said he would make a point of being more conscious about his posture the next time. And he was. Coachable moments like these are so important because the fact that it just happened makes the learning stay with the person longer.

Emotional Intelligence, or It's Not Just What You Say But How You Say It

To help someone learn and grow, to affect their self-knowledge and expand their experience, you have to be able to reach them effectively. That's where emotional intelligence comes in. By emotional intelligence I mean knowing how to read someone's reaction and speak candidly with empathy and an awareness of what will resonate most with that person. When it comes to delivering feedback, it means gauging in the moment how someone is reacting to what you are saying and making adjustments so they can better understand and accept it. If the person is becoming defensive, aggressive, or shutting down to what you have to say, you need to be able to pick up on that so you can work with it. You can be honest and fair while also being empathetic, and if you can do both at the same time, that can really help people process feedback that's uncomfortable to hear.

In fact, honesty, fairness, and empathy are the three qualities you're aiming for in tone or delivery when talking to someone. First, you have to be honest. It doesn't help anyone grow their knowledge or self-knowledge if you aren't giving it to them straight. Second, you need to make sure, as best you can, that you are being fair. That is why I suggest you prepare objective examples to back up what you say. You don't want your own feelings or biases, which we all have, to get in the way of constructive coaching. Third, you need to be empathetic. That means putting yourself in the person's shoes.

Feedback can be hard to hear. It can stir up insecurities. It can make someone feel disliked or undervalued. People take things personally. Sure, this is business, but it doesn't do you, the person, or your organization any good to pretend that a person's feelings can't enhance or hinder their performance.

Take the example I used above of the department head who was swaying back and forth during a presentation. I didn't just say, "You know, you looked like a see-saw up there swinging from one side to the other." I didn't say that because I first thought about how he might feel. This was a big presentation and thousand of people had been watching. If I came to him and said that he looked silly in front of everyone, he likely would have been embarrassed. Embarrassment tends to make people feel hurt or defensive, or both. It doesn't tend to make them feel open and willing to learn and change.

Instead, I started off with a compliment, not a criticism. After all, he had done one hundred things right and just one thing wrong. That is an important perspective for him to have. It also made him more receptive when I then pointed out the one thing he could do better next time. When I talked to him about that one thing, I didn't make fun of him or tell him he looked strange. Instead I focused on how he could come across in a more powerful and confident way the next time. That put him in the mind frame of imagining a more positive future moment rather than rehashing or worrying about what had just happened, something he could no longer do anything about. I also watched him reaction to determine if he needed more encouragement—if he had understood and accepted what I had to say. He accepted the feedback and was thankful for it, so there was no need to dwell on it any longer.

One of the best ways to develop empathy for others is to remind yourself of some of the more difficult or stinging moments that you have endured during your career. We have all had them, and even though most of us don't like to dwell on our less successful moments, they can be very educational. Review those moments in your mind and ask yourself: How did that moment make me feel? Did those feelings make it more difficult to learn from the experience? Was there something my leader could have said or done to help me process the feedback more constructively and get more out of the experience?

Remember, all leaders give feedback and do performance reviews. What we are trying to do here is give feedback in a better way, so the knowledge and information will stick. We are trying to take these common work processes to another level in order to give you an edge that a lot of leaders don't have. A lot of people don't like to think about or talk about people's feelings in the workplace because feelings are "unprofessional." But everyone has feelings and working with them instead of against them will simply make you more effective.

I have endured the discomfort of receiving tough feedback myself many times throughout my career. One recurring theme has been that I don't have to be so nice, that I should be tougher. The first few times I heard that, it was hard for me to accept, and I did little about it. That may have been because the leaders who talked to me about it only spoke in generalities, without tying them to specific experiences, so I didn't really connect with it. I started to realize it was something I truly needed to work on when I was at Burger King. The culture there was very combative, confrontational, and cutthroat. I was once in a meeting with the CEO and CMO along with about ten other people. I was presenting a plan for our global kids business, which I was responsible for, when the CEO and the CMO started arguing, loudly, with one another. These two had worked together for a long time. They liked and respected one another and this wasn't uncommon behavior for them. Still, I stayed out of it. That is until they stopped arguing, turned and looked directly at me, and asked, "What do you think?" I hesitated. "Is she right or am I right?" the CEO prompted. I didn't know what to say. I had a dotted line to the CMO but the CEO was the head of the company. I honestly didn't know how to answer, so I decided not to take a side. I told them, "Both of you are right, and both of you have fair points" and then I went on to explain why.

As soon as the meeting was over, my boss took me into a conference room. She said, "I'm going to give you some constructive coaching right now. If that ever happens again, you need to pick a side. It doesn't matter who you side with, you just need to tell people what you think and why. They want to see your conviction. They want to know where you stand and how much you believe in your idea. There was no right or wrong answer back there, but you should have picked a side." That coaching has stayed with me ever since. She was right, and I could see it right away. She didn't embarrass me in the room, but she did catch me right after, so the incident was still fresh. I was convinced, and I completely changed my approach. From that moment on, I have always told people what I think and show courage in my conviction.

Promote Know-How As A Priority

While feedback is about reviewing how someone has performed in the past, building know-how is about expanding someone's knowledge and skills for the future. As a leader, there is a lot you can do to make this something that people value and actively pursue.

Knowledge building is something you should think about for every one of your direct reports, especially your star performers. Someone like Employee B, who has already mastered so much in his current role, is in a perfect position to learn and grow into more responsibility. Whenever someone is in that High Potential/High Performance category, I always say the same thing: "It's extremely hard to get into that box, but it's very easy to get out of it. If you let down your guard, that's what will happen." I say that to get people thinking about how they are going to keep the momentum going, how they are going to build on their present success and keep raising the bar quarter after quarter.

Another way you can promote knowledge building is by encouraging team members to learn from one another. I'm all for healthy competition to get people to stretch themselves, but competition should not be prioritized to the point where people are keeping useful information or knowledge from their coworkers. You can help establish knowledge sharing as an important part of the culture by facilitating connections. When I'm providing feedback to people, I often look for ways to encourage them to network and learn more about other aspects of the organization. When you have a fuller picture of the business, when you get more viewpoints from more people, it makes it easier to connect the dots and better solve problems and innovate.

I often do this in a formal way by asking one team member to mentor another whom I believe can benefit from that person's experience. For example, when I was at Driven Brands, we bought a company called 1-800-Radiator. The president of that company had doubled the business in two years. I had someone in my department who was looking to grow his segment by a similar margin so I asked the president to mentor him because I thought his insight would be valuable.

I did something similar after I went on my "listening tour" at Maaco, which I talked about in the last chapter. By listening to our franchisees, I learned something that surprised me. In many of our markets, the franchisees didn't connect with one another very often. I figured they could learn a lot by simply sharing experiences, so I took steps to change that. I began by inviting groups of them out to dinner while I was in town to get them talking. Then I encouraged them to continue meeting, maybe on a monthly basis, after I was gone.

After I had been meeting with franchisees for about a month, I also started sending out a weekly blog as a way of communicating with everyone I had visited and sharing what I had learned. This helped spread the knowledge and insights I gained, and it showed that I cared enough about the business and these people to take the time to do so. My relationship with the franchisees, many of whom had been skeptical about me at first, changed rapidly for the better after that.

There's Always Something to Learn

The best organizations are the ones in which people take it upon themselves to learn as much as they can and make sure they are expanding their knowledge. Leaders can help facilitate these things, but we can only do so much. One of the best things we can do, however, is to surround ourselves with people who willingly take on the responsibility of learning and growing themselves.

There is always something to learn, even in the most difficult situations. Early on in my career, when I worked for my father's advertising agency in Venezuela, he purposely assigned me jobs that pushed me out of my comfort zone, believing that by challenging me, I would learn more about myself and my own resourcefulness. That proved true, but I also learned something about how *not* to lead when he put me to work for an account director who was the toughest boss in the company. He was the type who would yell at people in the hallways when he didn't get what he wanted or leave people crying at their desks after blistering assessments of their work. From him, I learned how a lack of humility and caring can make a leader pretty difficult to follow.

This lesson was crystallized for me one day when we had a meeting with an important client. Beforehand, as we were preparing, he said to me, "I don't want to be late, so I'm going to have the car pick us up for the meeting at exactly noon. Meet me downstairs at twelve on the dot." I understood the need to be on time, of course, so I did exactly as he instructed, but when I got to the lobby and looked around, I didn't see him. That's when someone told me that he had gotten in the car 10-15 minutes earlier, leaving me behind.

I suppose he was trying to teach me some kind of lesson, but what was it exactly? That I shouldn't follow his instructions? That I shouldn't believe what my boss says to me? That I shouldn't trust people, even if we were supposed to be on the same team? It felt like he had set me up for failure for no good reason, and I was determined not to give up so easily. In Venezuela, there are motorcycle taxis as well as cars, and the motorcycles tend to navigate Caracas traffic more quickly. The client was on the other side of town, so I jumped on the back of a motorcycle and arrived before my boss did in his car. When he walked into the conference room and saw me sitting there with the client, he looked furious but didn't say anything. As for me, I always remembered that moment. Some leaders confuse humility with humiliation, doing their best to beat people down and assert their authority over them. Other leaders adopt a humble position themselves and promote humility in others in order to show them how much room they have to grow, how much better they can be. I think it's pretty clear which one leads to better results.

That is what I learned from the experience. And it just goes to show you that you can get something out of every interaction. Hopefully, we are all better leaders than my old boss was, but I believe we can still communicate to our people the importance of looking at every experience, positive or negative, as an opportunity to learn.

Score Yourself on Leading Edge #1:
Gaining and Sharing Knowledge

For each of the questions that follow, answer Yes, No, or Sometimes. At the end of each section, add up the number of answers that fall in each of these three categories.

Gaining Knowledge

1. Are you able to keep your ego in check?

2. Can you admit when you're wrong or someone else has a better idea?

3. Would the people you work with describe you as open, approachable, and receptive?

4. Do you de-emphasize your position of authority?

5. Do you regularly look for ways to put yourself in other people's shoes and see the business from their perspective?

6. Do you willingly give credit to others for their ideas and accomplishments?

7. Do you take an active interest in people of all levels and departments?

8. Do you know how to ask good questions that spur conversation and allow knowledge to flow?

9. Are you a good listener even when the feedback is difficult to hear?

10. Are you able to listen in a way that makes people feel heard?

11. Are you an avid learner?

12. Are you open to learning more about yourself?

Sharing Knowledge

1. Do you provide people with regular, effective feedback that helps them improve on a regular basis?

2. Are your performance reviews simple and focused?

3. Do you provide fair and accurate feedback, even when it's hard to hear?

4. Do you help people internalize hard-to-hear feedback in a positive way?

5. Do you challenge top performers to do even better?

6. Do you offer proof and examples to back up and illustrate your feedback?

7. Do you focus on how people can improve personally as well as improve their business results?

8. Do you give people an opportunity to respond to your feedback about their performance?

9. Do you keep in regular touch with your direct reports so nothing in a performance review comes as a surprise to either of you?

10. Do you look for opportunities to provide spontaneous feedback?

11. When providing feedback, do you pay close attention to what you say and how you say it?

12. Do you regularly look for ways to help people to expand their learning and broaden their experience?

Score Yourself

Look back at each No or Sometimes answer that you gave. These are your areas of opportunity. Pick a few areas to work on, and over the next quarter think about ways that you can turn those Nos into Sometimes and those Sometimes into Yeses. Do this quarter after quarter, and it will be like you are doing performance reviews on your own leadership skills and abilities. Pay attention to how you change from quarter to quarter and how your gaining and sharing knowledge affects business results.

Your Top Five

Below, list five things you can work on over the next quarter to improve your score for Leading Edge #1: Gaining and Sharing Knowledge.

1.

2.

3.

4.

5.

LEADING EDGE #2: MODELING AND DRIVING EXPECTATIONS

3: Modeling Expectations—
Watch Your Shadow

When I first became a parent I noticed something that helped me a lot in terms of my effectiveness as a leader: My children are always watching me. All parents know what I mean by this. It often becomes obvious the first time you hear your child repeat something you said or imitate something you did. This happens despite the fact that you didn't consciously mean to teach those words or that behavior. Or you become aware when your child catches you *not* practicing what you have preached. This happened to me not long ago with my daughter. Our children are young, so my wife and I trade off taking them to the bathroom when we are out of the house. The other day we were out to dinner when my three-year-old said she needed to use the potty. I took her to the restroom, held the door for her, helped her on and off the potty – you know the drill. When we were finished, I went to the sink and washed my hands. I was heading for the door when she stopped me. "Papá, what about *my* hands?"

She had barely touched anything so I hadn't thought to wash

them, but she was absolutely right. My wife and I had been teaching her the importance of cleanliness and washing her hands regularly, and she had obviously heard us. She had heard us and she had caught me. In that moment, I wasn't acting as a good role model for the expectations we had set for her. Even when you aren't aware of it, children are paying attention, picking up your cues both good and bad. It's an awesome responsibility.

The same is true for the people you lead. This isn't to suggest that you treat your team members like children. Rather, you cultivate a greater awareness of the messages you are sending. And I don't just mean the messages you convey with your words when you are being intentional about it, as in a performance review or meeting, but the messages you send all the time. This is what I mean when I say *watch your shadow*. All leaders cast a shadow, whether they mean to or not, and that shadow affects how other employees think and behave. To lead with an edge, you have to become more conscious of the messages you send with your words and actions, in formal situations and informal ones, because people take them as clues to

- What is expected of them

- What you really care about

- What the organization really cares about

- How they can get ahead

- Whether they can trust you (i.e., whether you mean what you say)

This chapter is about learning how to make use of your shadow. With your words and actions, you can either send a message that reinforces the expectations you have for the people around you or undermines those expectations.

When Your Stated Expectations Don't Match Your Shadow

Suppose you have been trying to drive home the point to your direct reports that you want them to collaborate more, communicate more openly, to work more as a team instead of a collection of individuals in order to encourage greater knowledge sharing and innovation. You talk about the importance of this at every weekly meeting, and then, at the end of each meeting, you go directly to your office, shut the door, and focus on your work until the end of the day. You rarely meet people for lunch or take breaks in the common area. If people need something, you figure they can make an appointment with your assistant, even though your schedule tends to be pretty packed and they might have to wait awhile.

If this is the way you behave, what messages do you think people are truly getting from you? What messages are they getting about your stated objective of creating a more collaborative, team-oriented environment? Might they be thinking that there is one set of rules for them and another for you? Or that while teamwork sounds good, it isn't really that important? Or that you are yet another of the many hypocritical leaders out there who expect people to do as they say but not as they do? How effective do you think these kinds of messages are? Would you be persuaded or motivated by them? After all, you got ahead in this organization by not being very collaborative or team-oriented. So why should anyone else put in the effort if you don't?

I have a friend who once worked in an organization where a directive came down from the President himself that he wanted there to be more knowledge sharing. This came from the fact that there had been a couple of recent instances where one arm of the company knew something that another arm didn't. Different departments were wasting precious time and resources learning the same lessons that others already knew. The President was frustrated by this and told the members of the team that they needed to work on creating a more open environment where people from different disciplines interacted more and everyone was encouraged to contribute their knowledge and ideas.

Sounds like a good idea, right? The problem was that the leadership of this particular company had some longstanding habits that contradicted this new message. It was a culture in which people would get screamed at for not achieving a desired result or not having at hand the information the leader wanted. Leadership would do this publicly and often, humiliating team members in front of their peers. In fact, not a meeting went by without this happening at least once in order to "keep people on their toes," as one executive put it. The result was that most people kept their heads down and their mouths shut so as not to draw too much attention to themselves.

This dynamic continued even after the President had made a big point of highlighting at an all-staff meeting the problem we had been having of not sharing information. When another costly example of this happened about a month later, he was heard dressing down his entire team by yelling at them, "Why can't you [insert expletive here] people manage this simple task? Is it really that hard to talk to each other?"

This is what I call a *negative* or a *bad shadow,* and in this case it was being cast from the top of the pyramid. The President wanted more open communication, but because people found him so difficult to talk to, were even afraid to talk to him, it didn't happen very often no matter how much he wanted it. And because it was the President casting this kind of shadow, most of the senior leadership behaved the same way. So did their direct reports with their direct reports and so on down the line.

It's almost comical when you think about it. Here was a person who was basically screaming "Talk to me!" at the top of his lungs but didn't understand why people were running in the opposite direction. The reason was obvious from the outside, but he couldn't see it. I mean, who likes to be screamed at? No one on his senior team could see it either, or at least they weren't willing to speak up about it. Over the years I have kept a mental list of things I have seen leaders do that I never want to emulate; having such a profound lack of awareness about how people respond to me and why they respond that way is right up there at the top.

Practice Self-Awareness

It's important to keep in mind that people look to the leader for guidance and direction. Think of the leader's role like that of a lead actor's—on stage with an audience watching—only you are on stage practically all the time. As a leader, you project your expectations through your behavior, the words you choose, how you choose to communicate them, the way you dress, and your habits when it comes to things as common as email and phone calls. These are some of the things that cast a shadow. If your shadow projects a consistent and motivating message, then people are likely to follow it and you are likely to get the results you want. If not, expectations can become unclear and you can lose the respect of those around you.

If you are not getting the reaction or results you want or expect, it's important to look inward as well as out. Did someone simply fail to live up to your expectations, or did you send that person contra-dictory or unclear messages about what you expected? The more conscious you are of your shadow, the more you will be able to bring it into alignment with the message you intend to convey.

Creating this kind of alignment requires a high sense of self-awareness. Think about how much intention and preparation goes into getting ready to deliver a speech at a conference in front of an auditorium full of people. In a situation like that, you are likely to analyze everything—from what you plan to say and how long you plan to say it, to your tone of voice, what you will wear, your body language, how you will use the stage, whether you will be funny or serious, where and how long you will pause, whether you will use notes or a teleprompter or speak from the heart, and so on. You know that the impression you leave on people stems from a whole range of factors. The same is true in every interaction we have; we just don't tend to give most interactions nearly as much thought.

Now imagine if you *did* bring that kind of awareness into your daily interactions. If you think of yourself as being on stage, it's likely to change a lot about the way you think and act. Watching your shadow is often about monitoring the subtle cues you send to people, sometimes without even realizing it. Following are some basic areas to examine in order to gain a better understanding of the shadow you are casting and how to project a clearer, more effective message:

1) *How you dress*: At GrandVision, most of the leadership tries to be informal in a number of ways, including the way they dress. This is because the company wants to promote an anti-bureaucratic, non-hierarchical culture, one that allows us to be more nimble and move more quickly. As a result, much of our management team tends to dress down—no ties, no jackets, a more casual dress code—in order to reinforce this message and make ourselves appear more accessible.

That is a valuable shadow to cast and it's important to have self-awareness depending on the situation at hand. For example, if I'm meeting our Board of Directors, the media or investors, I always wear a suit and tie. I think good leaders know how and when to adapt their attire depending on the situation at hand. How you dress matters. It makes an impression on people, so make sure it's the impression you intend.

2) *Your email habits*: I've read that the average person gets hundreds of emails per day. It's such a ubiquitous tool that it's easy to get into mindless habits, to handle your emails without thinking too much about what message you are conveying as you do. But because email is such a big part of our daily work lives, it's a great place to show people what you care about and what you think of them. Some questions you might ask yourself before you hit the Send button include: Do my email habits show a respect for other people's time? Do they help people stay focused on what is most important to our organization?

You can answer these questions with a resounding yes if you make a point of being succinct in your emails and saving ongoing, long conversations for a different medium. I believe it's also important to avoid the Reply All button as much as possible, making sure to address messages only to those who need to read them, saving everyone else from unnecessary clutter in their inboxes. In *Unsubscribe*, author Jocelyn Glei writes about how email is killing our productivity, with the average employee spending 28 percent of the workweek managing messages, processing more than 120 of them each day. By simply being more intentional and efficient about the emails you send, you can show people how to avoid distractions and keep the focus on what really matters.

You also want to think about the language you use in your emails and apply the Golden Rule to the medium by asking yourself, Do I respond to people in the same way I want them to respond to me? Because people tend to email so often, they sometimes get into the habit of dashing off terse and less-than-thorough responses. Have you ever had the experience of asking three questions in an email only to get a response to one question in return? Or the response is so short and cryptic that it comes across as unhelpful, possibly even rude? If you have had such experiences and not enjoyed them, then make sure you aren't doing something similar in your replies.

3) *Your phone etiquette*: Who hasn't put off returning a phone call or a few calls because they were overwhelmed with other things? After all, the message stored on your voicemail is easier to ignore than whatever or whomever is right in front of you. But think for a moment about what that communicates to the person left hanging. Or, to put it another way, think about the last time someone didn't return your call. Did it make you feel like you were important to that person? Did it make you feel like what you had to say or what you were working on together was a priority for him or her? Probably not.

As a leader, you have to think about why you are doing something (i.e., I'm so busy, it will really help me out if I put this off until tomorrow) and how someone is going perceive those actions (i.e., your "why" must be clear or the person may think you don't care). Where you direct your time and attention signals to others what matters to you.

When I worked for Bernardo Hees, then CEO of Burger King, he used to say, "We don't have cash registers at the corporate office. Our cash registers are in every single one of our Burger Kings, and our franchise owners are the ones waking up every day generating our revenue." That is why I set a rule for myself that if a franchisee called me, I had to return that call within an hour. It was unacceptable to wait a day or more. Out of respect for the crucial role franchisees played in the success of our organization, I made sure that I was accessible to them and that my actions communicated how important they were. It was the same reason why, when we were onboarding new franchisees, I always gave them my business card with my office and cell numbers on it and told them, "If you need anything, you call my cell phone or text me. It doesn't matter what time of the day it is. If it's between midnight and five in the morning, I probably won't return your call right away, but any other time of day I will." They took me at my word, and I didn't give them any reason to doubt it.

4) *How you run meetings*: As with emails, meetings are a ubiquitous area of business where you can reinforce your expectations or undermine them. Do you show up on time? (If not, why should they?) Do you have a clear agenda? (If not, why should they be fully focused and attentive?) Does the meeting take only as much time as is needed to cover the agenda? Have you only invited the people who absolutely need to be there? Have you made sure your points are simple, straightforward, and limited in number? In short, do you display the kind of respectful, efficient, and productive behavior that you want from your employees each and every day?

You can model your expectations whether you are running the meeting or just participating. If someone else is speaking, you can show your interest by employing the same techniques I covered in chapter 1 in under the subhead Listening So Others Feel Heard. You can maintain eye contact, put your phone and laptop away, and let people finish before you start talking. If you are not fully listening and engaged, then you have to ask yourself: Is it really necessary for me to be here? Is it really necessary for any of us to be here?

5) *How you handle conflict*: Where there are people, there will inevitably be some friction and disagreements. That is to be expected and can even be a positive thing if handled well. In fact, the way a leader handles conflict conveys a lot.

For example, I was once in a meeting where a heated conversation broke out among about a dozen team members. We were discussing different ways to solve a particular problem, and one person suggested an idea that didn't resonate with the rest of the group. But, instead of allowing the conversation to move on, that person kept coming back to his idea and being confrontational, even argumentative, about it. I was addressing someone else in the room when this team member interrupted me. He wanted to bring up his idea once again even though it had been made clear, multiple times, by multiple people that no one else thought it was a good one. So I said, "Stop, I'm not talking about that anymore and I'm not talking to you right now."

I said this not just to make a point to the person who was interrupting me, but also for the benefit of everyone else in the room. I wanted them all to know that wasting time on ideas that had already been vetted and dismissed, that not listening to other people when they express their opinions, and that speaking disrespectfully by interrupting or bullying (which is basically what he was doing when he wouldn't take no for an answer), would not be tolerated.

Create Your Personal Board of Directors

Analyzing your own behavior to become more self-aware and more intentional about the signals you are sending is important, but it's not enough. We all have our own perspectives and we all have blind spots, which means it's impossible to see ourselves clearly. There are, however, some tactics you can use to guard against blind spots and expand your awareness. One of the most powerful ones I have come across is to put together your personal board of directors.

What is a personal board of directors? Exactly what it sounds like. All publicly traded companies and most private companies have a board of directors to help steer the ship. Why can't individuals have the same? You can. I have done it for years to help me grow as an individual and in my career.

The idea is to assemble a group of trusted, objective advisors who will help you see yourself clearly, expand your skills and thinking, and hold yourself accountable for the personal and organizational goals you set. Over the years, when I have presented the leadership program on which this book is based to different groups, I have consistently found that this is one of the most popular topics and the one that people have the most questions about no matter the industry, function, or level of experience. The response tells me that people are actively looking for ways to better understand how they can grow and get better at what they do. They just need help doing it. The following steps will help you get started in forming your personal board of directors.

1) *How to choose your board members*: In order to determine who will make the best mentors to include on your personal board of directors, you need to know what your long-term goals are. Begin by asking yourself the same kind of question you might get in a job interview: Where do I see myself in five to ten years?

Before I became group president at Driven Brands, I chose mentors who had risen to the level of president in their companies. I knew that was the position I wanted so I set my sights on people who had climbed similar ladders to that same height. They gave me insight into what the job was like and what I needed to do to get there.

Another question to ask yourself is, What skills am I lacking or where are my weak points? You might also look for board members who can help you broaden your knowledge and skills in key areas. For example, when I was at Burger King, 3G Capital, which owned a controlling stake in the company, was emphasizing the importance of change management. That was an area of business that I didn't know a lot about, so I looked to a former business school professor of mine from the University of Chicago. He was an expert in the field, and he taught me a lot about it. I talked with him about what our company was doing to manage change, and he helped me better understand the strategies and how I could participate in them more effectively.

A third and final question is, Who can help open doors for me and expand my network? You might choose someone higher up in your company, whose work you respect and admire, even if that person isn't in your department and doesn't hold a position you would want one day. If you are in marketing, for example, you might approach the CFO in order to gain a broader understanding of the business and expand your contacts within the company beyond those with whom you work on a regular basis. Or, if you are looking to move to another company, even another industry, someone who works there already would be a great choice to help you decide whether this kind of leap is right for you and to give you an in if it is.

Once you have asked yourself those three key questions, take a look at the list of names you have come up with. Ideally, certain candidates will fulfill more than one criterion. For example, the person who holds the position you hope to have one day may also be able to help you with critical skills you are lacking. Consider that as you narrow down your list, remembering to keep some backup options. You want to have a minimum of three and a maximum of five people on your board. Any fewer than three, and you don't have enough diversity of opinion or experience. Any more than five, and it's too much to handle. Always remember, these are relationships that will take time and effort to manage over the long term (more on that in the next section), so you don't want to become so overwhelmed by them that they become counterproductive.

One final consideration when assembling your list of candidates: Consider your professional and your personal growth. When you think about what will really give you an edge in life, maybe it has less to do with work and more to do with having a more grounded and mutually supportive marriage. Maybe you need to develop a more productive relationship with money and get better at setting and meeting your family's financial goals. Maybe you could use some help learning how to better manage your anger or stand up for yourself. These are the kinds of things that make us better people, and becoming better people can only help us become better professionals. Growth and success in one area tends to support growth and success in others (and vice versa: difficulty in one area of our lives tends to spill over into the rest). It's for this reason that I include Reverend Chip Edens, the rector of my family's church, on my personal board of directors. I go to him a lot to talk about things like family, faith, and giving back to my community, subjects that give me the grounding I need to go out and succeed in the world.

2) *How to approach potential board members*: The question of how to get someone to be a board member is one that many people are curious, even anxious, about. It can feel awkward to ask someone, especially someone you don't know, to take an active interest in your personal development. After all, it means an investment of time and energy on that person's part. That's why the first rule is to look for ways to give back. You want something from this person, but that doesn't mean the relationship has to be one-sided. You can always look for opportunities to make it worth your mentor's time as well as yours. With the professor from the University of Chicago, for example, I have spoken to his students and at the University's business school conference. For Reverend Chip Edens, I have taken part in community programs the church has sponsored and I'm always eager to help in any way possible. If you're not sure what you can offer someone, it's always a good policy to ask, Is there something I can do for you to return the favor?

Another useful tip is to take it slow. It's usually not a good idea to call up someone you don't know, out of the blue, and ask them for a regular mentoring appointment. Instead, start small. Let's say you work for Bank of America and you want to be mentored by the CEO or COO, someone whom you know has a busy schedule. Start by asking the person if he would be willing to grab lunch or coffee, or even spend just ten minutes with you in his office talking about your career and where it could be headed. Tell him that you admire his work and would find his perspective valuable (and don't forget to offer to return the favor in any way you can). Start with one meeting. If it goes well, ask if you can meet again sometime. If the person is willing, let the relationship evolve from there.

Nine times out of ten, people will say yes if you ask respectfully and make clear that you are asking because you respect and admire them. Of course, sometimes someone will say no, and that's okay. This is why it's a good idea to include backup options when you are making your list of candidates. Early in my career, I asked someone I admired to be my mentor. He agreed, but then when I showed up for three meetings in a row that he didn't seem prepared for or invested in, I cut my losses. I didn't take it personally. It may have been that he just didn't have the extra time to spend. Even though he was someone whose career I wanted to emulate in many ways, I figured my own time could be better spent with someone who was able to offer the attention and effort I was looking for.

Finally, consider making a financial investment in your board. There is a lot of useful advice available from professional consultants whose time you can pay for. If you are doing more and more public speaking at conferences and department-wide meetings, for example, a speech coach might be worth considering. In the past, I paid an executive coach to come to our offices, meet the people I would be working with, and ask them questions about me and about the organization. He came back with a lot of great insights that helped me hit the ground running. I saw it as a worthy investment in myself and my future.

3) *How to make the best use of your board members*: With some board

members, like a consultant whom you pay, the relationship will have defined objectives. With others, the relationship may be more informal. Either way, it's important to have an agenda of what you want to accomplish for every meeting. Depending on what sort of relationship you have established, you'll either inform your mentor up front about the agenda or follow his/her lead and work your agenda into the conversation.

With the University of Chicago professor, for example, we had a regular meeting once a month, and I told him specifically what I wanted to talk about and learn. With another CEO who once mentored me, I let him steer the conversation, but I always had a notebook with three to five key things that I wanted to ask about. I wouldn't set a formal agenda, but would make sure we covered those points during our conversation by saying something like, "The last time we met, we talked about the challenge I was having with retail marketing. I'd like to follow up on that." Because he had a more demanding schedule, I met him only once a quarter.

In other words, you can personalize your relationship with each board member so that it works for both of you. The number of times you meet each year, whether it's in person or by phone, whether the agenda is specified up front or not, and how formal or informal you are with one another are all flexible points depending on what is going to be most advantageous for both sides. One thing I would encourage you to do, however, is to make the meetings as regular as possible. Whether it's monthly, bimonthly, quarterly, or something else, try to get the sessions on the calendar early to make sure that you both follow through.

4) *How to keep your board fresh and relevant*: A personal board of directors is a tool I believe everyone can use throughout the entire course of their careers. However, your board will have to change as you change. After all, what you want and need today is not going to

be the same as what you want and need five or ten years from now. It stands to reason that the people who can help you realize those goals are not going to be the same either.

For example, early in my career a marketing professor was a very impactful part of my board. He worked with me for about ten years, and he is still a very good friend, but in terms of mentoring, I felt like I had gotten everything I could out of that relationship. I needed to move on and gain new perspectives so I transitioned him off my board and looked for someone new.

Now when this happened, I didn't go the guy and say, "We're done." That would have been disrespectful and dismissive of all the things he had done for me over the years. Instead, I made a gradual transition. We had been talking every month, so I suggested doing it quarterly instead. That allowed me extra time to search for a new candidate while still having the professor as a sounding board if I needed to. After that we moved to twice a year. Eventually, our contact evolved into an "every once in a while, as needed" situation, and that worked fine for both of us.

Top Five To-dos for a
Personal Board of Directors
That Will Give You a Leading Edge

1) **Target three to five people**: Any fewer and you won't have the benefit of a range of perspectives; any more and you have too many perspectives to consider—you don't want to have such a large board that you end up having to take time away from your job to manage the relationships and internalize the feedback.

2) **Make sure board members can help you realize your goals**: Think about what you want and what you need before choosing people to target. Think about how each person you are considering will help you fulfill those wants and needs.

3) **Meet regularly and with intention**: Make meetings a regular part of your schedule. Whether the agenda is loose or structured, make sure you give it some thought beforehand and come to each meeting prepared. Don't waste your board members' time or your own.

4) **Give back**: To sustain the relationship, keep it balanced. Look for ways you can give back to your board members. Giving back your time and talents in ways that can benefit your mutual interests.

5) **Keep evaluating your needs**: Your needs today and your needs five years from now are not going to be the same. Or, you may have gotten all you can out of a particular board member. Allow the relationships to evolve and your board to evolve so that you are always getting the most out of them.

Embrace Diversity

As the saying goes, "You don't know what you don't know." This is why tools like a personal board of directors can be so useful. Having a board means you are actively soliciting outside opinions about your work and yourself, which is what we all need to help us gain self-awareness and expand our knowledge and capability. However, since you are choosing your own board members, it's important to look closely at whom you are choosing and ask yourself if there is enough diversity of viewpoints among them. To put it bluntly, if you end up with people who think like you and agree with you most of the time, then you are not learning, growing, or expanding your awareness.

This is a crucial thing to consider in terms of who you choose for your board as well as who you recruit and hire, who you promote, and who you choose to surround yourself with on a regular basis. It's a natural human instinct to gravitate toward like-minded people from similar backgrounds. The problem with this is that it leads to a lack of diversity, which can be a real detriment to your success and that of your business for a whole array of reasons, including the fact that it can mean leaving top talent on the table, shutting yourself off from new ideas and innovations, and severely limiting your ability to learn, grow, and expand your perspective. If you surround yourself with people who think like you, act like you, and are from similar backgrounds, then you are also sending the wrong message: You are showing people that where you come from is more important than how good you are at your job.

Diversity is one of those buzzwords that we hear a lot about these days, but when I think about diversity in the workplace, I take a broad view. At Driven Brands, we had executives who came from a wide range of countries including the U.S., Cuba, Mexico, Ireland, and Venezuela (myself), so we were diverse in terms of nationality and ethnic backgrounds. But beyond that, I like to think about diversity in terms of different experiences, educations, and ways of thinking. For example, when I was at Burger King, we had someone with a background in engineering join our marketing team. He didn't have any marketing experience when he arrived, but he had other skills that the department was lacking; he was very process-oriented, analytical, and tech savvy. He has done so well in marketing since then that he is now Chief Brand Officer at one of the largest retailers in the US . In fact, he is one of the best marketers I know, and it never would have happened if leadership hadn't been willing to think outside the box. That would have been a real loss for him and for the company, which would have missed out on his unique perspective on marketing.

Of course, sometimes a more traditional view of diversity is important too. Recently, I was looking to bring someone new to my personal board of directors. When I took stock of the people I had chosen in the past and what new perspectives I might seek out I realized something important: I had never had a woman on my board.

I felt like that was a big oversight on my part, so I set my sights on a female board member who would also help me realize my goal of becoming a CEO of a publicly traded company one day. I did my homework and found someone who has had a long, successful career in the public sector, currently serves as a leadership consultant, and is on the board of directors of various public companies. She was outside my usual network of contacts, so I might not have found her had I not been specifically looking for more diversity. She hasn't been part of my board for long, but she has already had a profound influence on this leadership program you are reading about and my own leadership style. Since connecting with her, I have also realized my goal of becoming a CEO. That's not to say that she deserves all the credit, but she has certainly helped.

More Ways to Guard Against Blind Spots

Creating a personal board of directors is a great place to start, but there is more you can do. Following are some additional tools to guard against blind spots, increase your self-awareness, and ensure your shadow is projecting the message you intend:

1) *Record yourself:* A video recorder can be a powerful tool in this regard. It works especially well if you are giving a presentation or leading a meeting. Watching a recording of yourself will allow you to see yourself as others do and help you better analyze all the different signals you may be sending without even realizing it—from your facial expressions and body language to your rate of speech and use of pauses. But these aren't the only situations where recording is useful. I once took part in an ideation session for which a diverse group of people from finance, procurement, legal, marketing, and operations was brought together. We recorded the session so we could go back and see what ideas came out of it and which were worth following up on. An added benefit was that it allowed every-one who watched it to analyze the interactions. It was really educational to see what got people talking and what shut down conversation—when people took things personally and when they felt especially collaborative, when people were able to push through conflict and when they weren't. When you see the interactions on video, it takes some of the subjectivity out of your response. What's more, a couple of really good ideas came out of that session.

2) *Analyze other leaders*: Another great way to build awareness and enhance your message is to analyze leaders you admire. Think about leaders you know, or ones you have seen speak, and consider which ones left you with a strong impression. Spend some time

thinking about what they did to create that impression and whether there is something you can borrow from them.

There are also a lot of great online sources for leader speeches and interviews. I personally like *The David Rubenstein Show* on Bloom-berg.com, which features what they call peer-to-peer conversations about what makes a great leader. Rubenstein, co-founder of The Carlyle Group, talks with a diverse group of highly successful leaders like PepsiCo CEO Indra Nooyi, Nike co-founder Phil Knight, Comcast CEO Brian Roberts, Ret. Gen. David Petraeus, Microsoft co-founder Bill Gates, Berkshire Hathaway CEO and chairman Warren Buffet, and many others. As you watch these conversations, pay attention to what you respond to, either positively or negatively. Record your observations, then think about how they might apply to you and your shadow.

3) *Actively solicit opinions*: Don't just rely on your performance reviews and meetings with your board of directors. Everyone has an opinion, and you can usually find out what it is by simply asking for it. Ask for an opinion on what you are working on and an opinion about yourself. *How do you think I did during that presentation? What did you think about my idea to expand revenue? What do you think I'm missing in my analysis of this problem?* Questions like these followed with *I value your opinion, and I'd really like to hear what you think* can really open up discussions.

You know who gives me some of the toughest feedback? My wife, Cindy. We were in graduate school together, so honest feedback has been a valued part of our relationship for a long time. She knows me and she sees me, so when she is able to join me for a conference, she sits in the first row and observes me as I present. As soon as I come off the stage, she has feedback for me, like the time she told me that my reliance on a teleprompter was getting in my way. "You need to get so comfortable with your speech that you don't need a teleprompter because every time you look at it, it makes you seem unsure," she said to me. "It makes you look like a talking robot, like you don't know the content, when you are actually the expert." I watched the recording and could see what she meant. I didn't stop using a teleprompter right away, but I practiced and worked up to it. Now when I'm onstage, I just talk to the audience. Not only am I better able to connect with people that way, it makes me feel more confident even if I don't say everything perfectly.

Deliver Your Message with Consistency and Positivity

Oftentimes people just act the way they act. They don't think about what they are projecting to others. But once you are aware of your shadow and you have some tools to help to see it clearly, you can really be intentional about the message you want to convey.

Ask yourself what key messages you want to communicate as a leader. One of the main ones for me when I was at Driven Brands was growth. Regardless of someone's role in our company, I wanted that person to be thinking *growth, growth, growth,* continuous improvement, and continuous performance, whether that meant top-line sales growth, franchisee profitability growth, increasing unit count, increasing resource efficiency, and even personal growth among our team members. In order to ensure that the message was being received, it needed to be conveyed with focus and consistency. When I left Driven Brands, we had sixty months of consecutive same-center sales growth. We kept track of that number and made it known every month. In fact, I talked about it all the time because it was a trend we wanted to continue. I wanted everyone to be worried that at some point we might have to start the count over from zero.

You are casting your shadow all the time, so consistency is key, but so is positivity. When you have stellar results like that, I believe you want to bang the tambourine and yell it from the rooftops over and over again to drive the point home. When you have a negative you need to convey, you need to be more cautious. If things need to change, if performance isn't cutting it, you need to make sure people understand that message. But if you talk about it too often, when you overdo it, then people can feel like they are being beaten while they're down and the effect will be less motivation instead of more. Overkill brings morale down, and that is the last thing any leader wants in any circumstance—especially a difficult one.

Watching your shadow is about beginning to create a culture of accountability (a subject I will talk a lot more about in chapter 8). If I'm doing it, my team has to too. If my team members do it, then their team members have to too. If this is the standard I'm holding myself to, then others should expect to be held to the same standard. It's about sending a clear, consistent message about what it takes to succeed. In the next chapter, I will talk about how best to reward that success so you can continue to gain that edge.

4: Driving Expectations—Set Clear Goals and Challenges

The last chapter was about gaining self-awareness as a leader—about really seeing who you are and what you are projecting to people so that you can lead by example. Any one of us is a leader only so long as people agree to follow us, so if you don't start from a place of walking the talk, of practicing what you preach, of holding yourself to the same high expectations you set for others, then you undermine your credibility from the start. It's not that complicated. Ask yourself: Would I want to follow a leader who says one thing and does another?

Modeling expectations is important but it's not enough. You also have to set expectations for others and create conditions where those expectations can be achieved. All leaders do this to some degree, but leaders with edge make sure to set the bar high (yet not so high that people feel like they can't reach it) and help people grow and stretch their boundaries (for their own sake and for the sake of the organization). It's the job of leaders to keep the focus on growth and continuous improvement on every level—for themselves, for each of their direct reports, collectively as a team, as a department, and as an organization.

Promote A No-Surprises Culture—Clear, No-Nonsense Goals

Earlier in my career, I became VP of marketing for Burger King at a time when the business was really struggling in key markets. When I was interviewing for the position, Bernardo Hees, then CEO of the company, told me about the problems and opportunities that would come with the position and then asked me three basic questions— about my background as an entrepreneur, about how I had weathered the recent recession, and about what I would do to grow the business at Burger King. That was it. It took all of ten minutes to talk those things through, and then he made me an offer on the spot.

Along with that offer, however, came a clear and bold directive: "It will be your responsibility to turn around the Mexico business unit," Hees told me. "They have been negative for more than thirty-six months. You have six months to turn things around or I'll fire you."

Hees was an amicable, friendly guy most of the time, but he didn't beat around the bush. He was clear about what he expected from people, and he was clear in how he communicated that to them, leaving no room for ambiguity. Those qualities helped him do several critical things that every leader could learn from:

1) *Get people's attention*: There can be a lot of noise in business—a lot of conflicting messages and changing agendas. If a leader can cut through that noise and keep people focused on what matters, that is a huge edge. I didn't know Hees all that well, so at first I was a little bit shocked by the directness of his challenge. But it certainly got my

attention. Then, once I let it sink in and really thought about it, I found it refreshing and motivating.

2) *Make sure people understand what is expected of them*: The honest and direct way that Hees communicated his expectations made me think long and hard about whether I really wanted this position and believed I could accomplish what he needed. I'm a competitive person by nature, someone who doesn't like to fail, and taking the position meant I would have to leave the marketing agency I had started, which was doing quite well at the time. Did I really want to give up a good thing to work in a business that had been struggling for such a long time?

I like a challenge, and Hees made it clear that what he was offering me was a big challenge. I believed I could live up to his expectations, so I took the job. Because I knew exactly how my success was going to be measured, I immediately trained my focus on the goal of turning around our business in Mexico. On day one, instead of showing up at corporate headquarters in Florida, I went straight to the office in Mexico City. I was against the clock and I knew it, and that drove my behavior from the outset. And it worked. Within just six weeks, the Mexico numbers were already turning positive. And they were still positive twenty-eight months later when I left the company.

3) *Show people how they can get ahead*: In that interview, Hees didn't just tell me what he expected of me. He also laid out how I would be rewarded if I succeeded. He talked about the company's incentive program, and how I could climb the corporate ladder if that was what I wanted to do. Later, he followed through on those promises. Along the way, I got different rewards and promotions that were consistent with the numbers I was delivering. Later in this book I will talk more about building a culture of meritocracy and reward-

ing success, but for now, remember the lessons of the last chapter. If you want people to follow you, they have to believe in you and trust that you mean what you say. When I met the expectations Hees set for me, I was rewarded. When I exceeded them, I was rewarded even more. Clear. Direct. No surprises. No regrets.

Ask Yourself

Does every single one of my direct reports know exactly what they need to do to succeed? Does every single one of my direct reports' direct reports know what they need to do to succeed? Is everyone crystal clear on their goals and how those goals contribute to the growth of the company? If you aren't sure of the answer to any of these questions, ask people to articulate their goals for you.

Taking the time to set clear, no-nonsense goals is one of the best ways to drive success. It promotes a real awareness among your team members so they understand how to measure their own worth, particularly when you pair it with the kind of regular feedback and knowledge building I discussed in the first section of this book. It means people can see the progress they are making and the value they have to the company at all times. It keeps them focused on the things that will truly grow the company and motivates them to stay that course. This is the advantage of building a no-surprises culture in which no one ever has to guess what they need to do or where they stand at any given time. It's the leader's job to make goals and expectations as clear and simple as possible so that team members can focus their time and energy on achieving real results—not on trying to figure out what they should be doing next to get ahead.

Promote A Think-Big Culture — Stretch Goals and High Expectations

Another thing that Hees did that was effective was to set the bar high. He didn't just tell me I needed to grow the business by ten percent over the next two quarters; he told me I needed to turn it around completely. It was a very aggressive goal, the kind that business consultant and author Jim Collins would call a "big, hairy, audacious goal." This is where a leader can really help people grow, stretch themselves, and figure out what they are truly capable of.

These kinds of expectations are important because they can change the way people think. At GrandVision, for example, whenever we set our budget and projections for the coming year, we set our objectives so far above and beyond that they almost seem unreachable. That can mean that we fall as much as five percent short of our goal, but we still come out ahead. Why? Because if we had set our sights on growing by a modest ten or fifteen percent, then when we reached that point, we would have all felt pretty good about ourselves and probably become a little complacent.

Instead, we actively guard against complacency and promote a growth-focused mind-set when we say, "Our goal is to double our business." Even when we fall short of that goal, we still do far better than a modest fifteen percent gain. This can work in any business to change the way people think about what's possible. At one company I worked for, we doubled the size of the company in two years. When I left, we were on track to double it again in the next two years. Think about that for a moment: for a company to be able to transform in such a way that it doubles its profits and then doubles them again is hugely significant. It never would have happened it if we hadn't started out with some truly big and bold expectations.

This kind of goal setting can change the way people think. Instead of aiming for incremental progress, they start to come up with ideas for making big, impactful changes. They begin to question basic assumptions and look more closely at the ways in which the business works. That is what I did when Hees set the clear and aggressive goal for me of turning the business around in six months. There was a sense of urgency that drove my actions. I started off by immediately combing through the research and consumer insights to get a better understanding of the problems that Burger King was facing. What my team and I discovered by looking at the data was that Mexico had gotten off course by trying to follow our U.S. marketing strategy. In the U.S., Burger King had developed an irreverent, discount-based ad campaign aimed at eighteen- to twenty-four-year-old males. Mexico tried to follow that lead, but the strategy didn't suit the customer base.

Research showed that in Mexico, Burger King was less of a destination for young men on the go and more of a place where families went for a meal together. Those customers wanted a comfortable and satisfying dining experience and were less concerned about getting a quick bite at a bargain price. In further contrast to the U.S. customer, Mexican customers didn't use the drive-through all that often, and they were willing to pay more for quality. After we digested that research, we weren't interested in making small, incremental changes over time. We changed our strategy completely and implemented those changes as quickly as we could.

Along with my team, I developed an immediate action plan for the first ninety days that incorporated changes to nearly every aspect of the business. Our plan reflected new views around pricing, product, advertising, communication, and brand positioning. Among the things we did was to actually raise prices, offering a full meal, including dessert, at a mid-range price point that appealed to our more mature customer base. We added more menu options and completely changed our advertising to target families, partnering with brands like Xbox, the producers of *Spiderman* and *The Jungle*

Book, and music celebrities to draw in more kids and teens as well as their parents. There was no time to waste, so we started making these changes during my second week on the job.

Looking to do more than simply make improvements — we need-ed to turn around the business completely, or at least I did if I wanted to keep my job — made all the difference in our success. We were focused on moving fast and having a big impact. And we accom-plished just that. Remember, we went from more than thirty-six months of negative numbers to more than twenty-eight months of consecutive same-store sales growth, which is a pretty remarkable improvement.

Challenge People to Grow and Stretch

Sometimes leaders need to give their people a push in order to help them grow. Of course, a push can mean different things for different individuals. To do this effectively, you need to employ some of the tactics I talked about in chapter 1. If you have been doing the work of getting to know your people and building relationships with them, then you will have a much better sense of how best to challenge them. You want to look for challenges that are going to push people out of their comfort zones, but not stump them or leave them feeling stranded. You want to set them up with challenges that are going to excite and inspire them because that is going to make it much more likely that they, and by extension the organization, will succeed in a big way. The more you know about a person, the better able you will be to push them in the right direction.

I once worked with a smart, young analytic accountant who was doing very well in his role. When I got to know him better, I learned that he didn't see himself working in accounting for the rest of his life. This wasn't something that he was talking about all that openly. He never said outright, "I'm feeling a bit confined by my current position, and I'm not sure it's the right place for me." Instead, it came out when I asked him where he saw himself down the line. "Well, I'd like to grow and take on new roles, but I don't think I'm interested in becoming chief financial officer one day." That was interesting information to me because if he was looking the climb the corporate ladder, which he clearly was, CFO would have been the most logical end goal.

Curious, I asked him, "What would you like to do instead?" Right away he answered, "I've been thinking about trying my hand at operations."

Going from accounting to operations is an unusual shift to make in any organization. However, it was clear to me that this was a smart, resourceful, and driven young man. His ability to grow and affect the company was likely to be negatively impacted if he wasn't truly happy where he was. After talking with him a few more times to make sure he was confident about his decision to change the course of his career, I presented him with a challenge: I had been looking for someone to run procurement for one of our top brands, and I wanted to know if he would like to give it a try.

The new position meant he would have to learn a whole new area of the business. One hundred million dollars of transactions went through that department at the time, so he would be taking on a lot of responsibility as well. In the same way that Hees had once done for me, I made the challenges and expectations of the new role clear to him. He was excited by the prospect and readily accepted the challenge.

After six months in the posi-

> **Ask Yourself**
>
> What is going to inspire my people to go the extra mile? What is going to inspire them to push themselves to really find out what they are capable of?

tion, my new head of procurement was doing a phenomenal job. He was a great example of how, if a leader takes the time to get to know someone, asks the right questions, and gains a thorough understanding of the person's strengths and opportunities, a strategic chance can pay off in a big way.

Take Responsibility for Other People's Success

A crucial part of challenging people and setting high expectations is to then support them and make sure they have what they need to succeed. If you don't do this, your people will begin to feel like they are being set up to fail, and that is a sure way to discourage people and lose their trust. The following tactics are ways to help you continue to drive expectations and conditions for those high expectations to be met time and time again.

Tactic #1: follow up and follow through: When you challenge people, you are putting added pressure on them to expand their capabilities and perform beyond what has previously been expected of them. When Hees challenged me, I was used to that kind of pressure. In fact, I was the one who usually put pressure on myself to succeed. But that is not always going to true for everyone. And if someone falls behind, it can affect the whole team, even the whole organization. If you want someone to meet high expectations, you have to start with the kind of clarity that I talked about in the beginning of this chapter. Then you have to follow that up with regular contact in order make sure the goal remains clear and the person is staying on track to achieve it. This kind of consistency is the real day-to-day work of every leader with an edge.

Let's say, for example, that I have a team member who doesn't show a high degree of personal drive. When this type of team member is tasked to work under pressure to meet a deadline, then I adopt a specific strategy to keep the pressure on. This is a clear departure from my typical management style, but in certain cases, you have to adapt your approach. If he is working on a high-priority project with a tight end-of-the-day deadline, I will make sure to walk by his desk first thing in the morning to check in. I will say something like: "Hey, how's going? Do you have everything you need to make this happen? Do you need any help from me or anyone else? I'm sure I don't have to remind you how important this is, and we need it by 5:00 p.m., so anything you need to make that happen, or anything that is getting in the way of that happening, you be sure to let me know right away."

Then I will follow up with an email around ten o'clock to get a progress report. Around noon, I will say, "I'm going downstairs to get lunch. Can I bring you something so you don't have to interrupt your work?" Depending on the progress I have seen him make thus far, I may be back up at his desk at one. I will keep up the pressure by checking in every hour or two until he gets the message or gets the project done. I don't think you have to be a jerk about it, but you do have to show up to make sure your expectations are being met. You also have to provide guidance or assistance as needed. After all, the main objective is to get the work done and for everyone to succeed—not to catch someone falling behind or failing.

When I was at Burger King, we had an open office concept, where everyone sat at desks in a wide open space. There were very few doors anywhere in the office that could be closed, which made it easy for me and other leaders to manage people by walking around—to notice what was getting done and how people were reacting to things. I'm a fan of this sort of office setup for that reason, but regardless of your work environment, you need to find a way to follow up with people. The higher the expectations you have for people, the more important this becomes.

Tactic #2: Prioritize personal drive in hiring: You will decrease the amount of time you need to spend checking in and following up with people if you make personal drive a key factor in your hiring decisions. Let's say you are deciding between two candidates: A and B. They have similar résumés, but one has exhibited personal drive— the ability to motivate herself and follow through on her objectives— while the other is the kind of person who needs to be told what to do and monitored closely. Candidate A is the person I will hire 100 percent of the time. Personal drive is so important that I would consider hiring candidate A even if her résumé wasn't quite as good as candidate B's. If someone has the drive, she can quickly make up what she may lack in experience, but personal drive is harder for a leader to teach without putting in a lot of extra time and effort.

Personal drive is something I learned from my parents and grandparents. My grandparents on both sides were immigrants and entrepreneurs, and my dad is an entrepreneur so they taught me by example. Successful entrepreneurs have to put a lot of pressure on themselves to succeed because they don't have a choice. It's their business, their dream, and they have to be the driving force to make it work. I grew up in a household of people who emigrated from Europe to Venezuela with little more than what they could carry in a single suitcase. My grandparents and my father built their businesses from nothing. Their drive to succeed, paired with a willingness to work hard (something I will talk more about in the last section of this book) was practically all they had to offer in the beginning. When I'm interviewing people, I try to find that quality in them because I know firsthand what a difference it can make—in a person's life and in the success of a business. It's not to be underestimated.

Tactic #3: Make goals and results public: Transparency is a key factor in driving expectations and results based on those expectations. After all, if you are going to be held to very high standards, don't you want to know that everyone else is too? When team members start to think that they are being unfairly singled out or that more is expected of them than others, that is when their engagement and motivation starts to wane. That is the opposite of what you want in a high-performance culture. Oftentimes people feel that way because they simply aren't fully aware of the pressure being put on others, which is a situation that can be quite easy to remedy.

At Burger King, we made everything public. The quarterly key performance indicators (KPIs) and performance reviews of every employee, including the CEO, were posted on the wall of our open-concept office for everyone to see. Of course, we also tracked progress toward those KPIs on a regular basis. The data we used for tracking was obviously different depending on a person's role. It might be a daily or weekly sales figure. It might be the number of customer complaints in a month. It might be the number of new units opened in a quarter. Whatever it was, we would collect the data and use it to rank everyone within each department. And then we made those rankings public.

This was another way of ensuring that everyone knew, at all times, exactly where they stood within the company and in comparison to their peers. When you publicly rank people like this, one of two things typically happens with low performers: Either they are motivated to improve so they don't continue to end up at the bottom of the list, or they start polishing their résumés so they can find a new job. Either outcome is a good one from a leader's perspective. Those with potential are motivated to up their game, and those without much potential are motivated to manage themselves out of the organization, saving you the trouble of doing it yourself and opening up space for new talent.

Tactic #4: Make your own goals and results public: We talked about this in last chapter, but it's important enough to reiterate: You have to lead by example. If the goals and results of your team are important enough to make public, then yours are too. At Burger King, my KPIs were posted on the wall alongside those of every person under me. At every all-employee meeting, the first slide we shared showed the results of the entire company so everyone could see where the top leaders stood and also how their own goals were contributing to the success of the whole. The KPIs of the CEO and each member of the executive team were shared with our directors at every board meeting. Our results were not only public; we drew attention to them on a regular basis. That reinforced the idea that high expectations applied equally to everyone in the company.

Tactic #5: Sometimes people have to go: If you have been clear and transparent about people's goals and results, then it should come as no surprise if someone has to go. They will have seen clearly that they haven't been hitting the mark. You will have given them a chance to improve and they will have failed, not just once but over time. As uncomfortable as it can be, it's crucial that leaders manage out those who don't meet high expectations (more on how to do this effectively in chapter 6) — for the sake of the person who is failing and for the sake of everyone else.

Who stays and who goes in an organization is a clear indication of what is expected of people. If you set big, hairy, audacious goals and foster high expectations, but there are no consequences for someone who doesn't rise to meet them, it sends a message to everyone that those expectations really don't matter all that much.

To a certain extent, you want to make the culture around you a little bit polarizing. People either love it or they hate it. They either want to work there or they don't. There is nothing to be gained from letting people exist under the radar and not have to show themselves or show their dedication to the business. People need to know that they have to work hard in order to get a raise or a promotion. It may be easier and more comfortable to give everyone a cost-of-living increase every year than to separate people by merit and reward them accordingly, but it's never going to be as effective in inspiring people to get the results you are aiming for.

Sometimes You Need to Recalibrate

It's critical to track results on a regular basis, so you can publicly post people's results and to make sure the goals you have set are attainable. One of the crucial jobs of a leader is to make sure you are setting the right goals for people—the kind that will lead to the results the organization needs. Stretch goals are motivating and can separate those who have personal drive and who belong in the organization from those who don't. Impossible goals, however, can undermine people's confidence in themselves and their leaders. They can be absolutely devastating, especially to people with high personal drive.

This means that one of the main responsibilities of a leader is to set goals and keep calibrating to make sure you are on the right track. At Burger King, our management team once set the stretch goal of opening one hundred locations in a year. We were really excited about this vision because we had forecasted how much more business we could do with the additional locations. Of course, we then tracked our progress. If you do the math, having one hundred new locations by the end of the year meant we needed to open stores at a rate of eight or nine each month. Our first month, we missed the mark. But we were just getting started so we kept trying. In our second month, we missed our target again. At that point we stepped back and started asking questions. Why hadn't we been able to reach our goal? Did we have a pipeline problem? Was it an issue with real estate? Was the permitting process or some other internal process too slow to meet our goal?

To continue pushing toward that goal without making adjustments would have been counterproductive. That's why it's so important to keep on top of the progress people are making—or not making—so you can identify what is getting in the way. Is it the person tasked with achieving the goal, or is it something else that person has little control over? Our main objective for Burger King never changed, but we did have to slow down our timeline and set some additional goals for improving and speeding up our processes before we could hope to achieve our vision of one hundred new restaurants in a year. Business isn't static, so goals can't be either. They are things that need to be constantly monitored, tweaked, and improved upon to make sure they work.

Think about the impact on people if you don't do this right. As we will talk about later in the book, an employee's compensation should closely correlate to results. Bonuses, raises, and promotions should all be tied to performance. But if the leader has set unattainable goals, then people can work really, really hard and still not reach the point where they receive a bonus or promotion. They won't reach it because they can't reach it. People won't stick around if that happens too often, and the last thing any leader wants is for good people to be driven out the door by ill-conceived expectations.

Be Aware of Team Member Expectations

As a final word, leaders should keep in mind that they aren't the only ones who have expectations. If you want your people to strive to meet your high expectations, you really have to be thinking about whether you and your company are meeting their expectations.

The best way to do this is to establish a culture of open communication. At meetings, both one-on-ones and group meetings, even in interviews, it's important to encourage questions and feedback.

You have to ask for it. Don't just assume people will speak up if they have concerns. Then there are other methods like suggestion boxes and employee satisfaction surveys, which can be anonymous for people who are worried about the negative consequences of speaking up. Some of the informal get-togethers I talked about in the first section—like bagel breakfasts or beer Fridays—can be great settings for encouraging people to be more open and honest.

Inviting feedback from employees and taking it seriously doesn't mean that you aren't a strong leader or that you are letting your people dictate the course of business. In fact, you may not change a thing about the goals and expectations you set as a result. What it does is give you more information you can use to make sure everyone is on track and focused on the same end game. You can't solve problems if you don't know what they are, and employees who are unhappy, uninvested, and unengaged can definitely be a problem.

At GrandVision, we have a lot of young employees, and I personally interview ten to fifteen millennials a week as potential new hires. I always ask what matters most to them when choosing a company to work for, and time and time again I hear that they want a nimble, flexible environment to work in. They want opportunities to move, learn, and grow. They might work for the company for two to five years and then take what they learned to another organization where they could gain different kinds of experiences. That's a big change from previous generations that were more often looking for stability in a place they might stay at for the course of their career.

This kind of information is highly useful for a leader. It might cause you to make process and structural changes to adapt to these young people's expectations—perhaps by offering more movement among departments, or by having performance reviews more often so that people can get promoted quicker if they deserve it. But be on the lookout for ways to manage outsized expectations. Sometimes people are looking for growth before they have earned it, or they move to a position that really doesn't suit them. If you are aware of this, then you can do something about it. With some employees who wanted advancement before they were ready, I would offer them a business challenge and monitor them closely throughout the duration of the project. I might say, "Fix this process within six months, and I will move you up the ladder." If they succeeded, then great. If they didn't, then they knew why and had a clearer sense of how much they still needed to learn. With others, I might offer them a lateral move so they would still get a chance to grow their skills and experiences even if they weren't getting a raise or taking on more responsibility.

A continuous feedback loop is the best way to get your expectations met and to meet those of the people you lead: You can be clear and honest with them, and they can be clear an honest with you. If nothing else, just making sure people feel heard can go a long way in making them feel invested in the company and its goals.

Score Yourself on Leading Edge #2: Modeling and Driving Expectations

For each of the questions that follow, answer Yes, No, or Sometimes. At the end of each section, add up the number of answers that fall in each of these three categories.

Modeling Expectations

1. Would the people around you describe you as someone who leads by example, who practices what you preach?

2. Do you have a high degree of self-awareness about how others see you and about the messages you project to others?

3. Are you aware of the messages you are projecting in the way you dress?

4. Are you aware of the messages you are projecting when you email people?

5. Are you aware of the messages you are projecting through your phone etiquette?

6. Are you aware of the messages you are projecting when you run or attend meetings?

7. Are you aware of the messages you are projecting when you are confronted with conflict?

8. Do you regularly work to gain greater self-awareness and guard against blind spots?

9. Do you actively solicit opinions about yourself and your work in formal ways (like a personal board of directors) and informal ones (by simply asking people for their opinions)?

10. Do you strive to surround yourself with a diversity of opinions and perspectives?

11. Is the message you are projecting to people a consistent message?

12. Is the message you are projecting to people a positive message that they will want to follow?

Driving Expectations

1. Is every single person under you aware of your expectations for him or her?

2. Are you able to set goals for people that are absolutely clear and consistent?

3. Are you able to set goals for people that help them stretch themselves and grow both personally and professionally?

4. Have you gotten to know your people well enough to understand how best to challenge them?

5. Do you regularly offer people opportunities to challenge themselves?

6. Do you consider it your responsibility to do everything you can to ensure your people meet their goals and live up to your expectations?

7. Do you follow through to make sure people have what they need to succeed?

8. Do you prioritize personal drive when hiring or promoting people?

9. Do you make the goals and results of your team members transparent to all?

10. Do you make your own goals and results transparent to all?

11. Do you monitor and recalibrate the goals you have set for others to ensure that they are the best and right ones?

12. Are you aware of the expectations your team members have of you?

Score Yourself

Look back at each No or Sometimes answer that you gave. These are your areas of opportunity. Pick a few areas to work on, and over the next quarter think about ways that you can turn those Nos into Sometimes and those Sometimes into Yeses. Do this quarter after quarter, and it will be like you are doing performance reviews on your own leadership skills and abilities. Pay attention to how you change from quarter to quarter and how modeling and driving expectations affects business results.

Your Top Five

Below, list five things you can work on over the next quarter to improve your score for Leading Edge #2: Modeling and Driving Expectations.

1.

2.

3.

4.

5.

LEADING EDGE #3:
DREAM BIG, WORK HARD

5: Dream Big—Inspire and Motivate

I first heard the phrase *Dream big, work hard* from 3G Capital, the Brazilian private equity firm that acquired Burger King just prior to me working there. It was a concept that I brought to GrandVision when I became CEO to describe the ambitious, performance-based culture we were striving for. Jorge Paulo Lemann, one of the founders of 3G, always used to say, "To have a big dream requires the same effort as having a small dream. Dream big!"

Here, I use the phrase *Dream big* to talk about what you can do as a leader to inspire and motivate your people. You are in a position to help them dream big and pursue those dreams, for themselves and for the organization. People will feel more engaged, more invested in the success of the company if they feel like their own dreams are allowed to flourish there. And of course they should be, because inspired employees are an asset to any organization.

Psychologists Todd M. Thrash and Andrew J. Elliot have studied the topic of inspiration, and their research was featured in an article for *Harvard Business Review* ("Why Inspiration Matters" by Scott Barry

Kaufman, November 8, 2011). They found that inspired people tend to have certain key attributes, among which are that inspired people are more

- Absorbed in their work

- Driven to excel at their work

- Self-motivated (more of that personal drive I talked about in the last section)

- Optimistic about outcomes and their own abilities

- Open to new experiences

In other words, inspired employees are employees with an edge, which is why it's so important for leaders to know how to tap into the power of inspiration.

The Problem with Leading by Intimidation

There are good reasons why engagement numbers are so consistently low from year to year throughout the business world. Inspiring people to care enough to work hard for your organization is hard work in and of itself. And yet, far too many leaders waste their time and energy going about it in ways that just don't work. For example, not long ago a friend shared with me the following email from an executive at the high-profile tech company where she works:

Open letter to all employees:

At our all-staff meeting last week, I addressed the question of what's going to happen now that we have been bought by another firm. Despite taking the time to do that, I have been made aware that your questions and speculations have continued without abatement. So let me put an end to them right now. The only thing any of you need to be worrying about is how well you are doing your jobs. The only thing any of you need to be asking about is how you can do your jobs better. Anything other than that is simply beyond your pay grade, so let's all stop with the gossiping and bellyaching and focus on what we need to do to meet the demands of our new owners. After all, that is our primary objective.

When there is something to know, you will be told. If changes are coming, you will have to adjust. If you can't live with that and are going to continue to be distracted by questions surrounding our new ownership, then you should do us all a favor and leave now.

Everyone needs to be on notice: I will not spend one more minute coddling people or allaying their fears. Nor will any member of the leadership team. The next person who brings up the subject might as well hand over his or her resignation letter at the same time. Enough is enough. Get back to work.

I wish I could say I was surprised by what I read, but I have witnessed similar tactics far too often throughout my career. I have had supervisors and colleagues who behaved in similar ways, using threats, embarrassment, and other negative tactics to try to motivate people. In fact, this kind of intimidation is pretty common in today's business world.

While I'm certainly not against putting pressure on people, too often what leaders call pressure or straight talk is really nothing more than bullying. And the crucial question in my mind is this: Are intimidation tactics like these really all that effective?

My personal experience leads me to say no, and research backs up my conclusion. As Robert I. Sutton, professor of management science and engineering at the Stanford School of Engineering, put it in an article for *McKinsey Quarterly* ("Memo to the CEO: Are you the source of workplace dysfunction?" September 2017): "Hundreds of experiments show that encounters with rude, insulting, and demeaning people undermine others' performance, including their decision-making skills, productivity, creativity, and willingness to work harder and help coworkers." His conclusion was that it's the leader's job, not to strike the sort of rude and dismissive tone obvious in the above email, but to actively guard against it. Or, as he put it more succinctly: "Your job is to build an organization where jerks don't thrive."

I have seen instances where people were initially motivated by intimidation to step up their game, but I have never seen that motivation last for very long—particularly not among your best and brightest people. The employee who showed me the email confided that after it made the rounds, a number of her colleagues had quietly begun searching for new jobs, including her. In fact, that was why she had reached out to me in the first place—to find out if I had any good leads for her. She and her coworkers felt their concerns were being dismissed and that their livelihoods were in jeopardy. Since this leader did nothing to reassure them, why would they stay if they had other options?

What's more, my friend said that no one talks to this leader anymore unless it's absolutely necessary. That means he has cut himself off from the knowledge, ideas, and feedback he is going need if he wants to accomplish what he said was his primary objective—to meet the demands of the new parent company. If the point of his email was to isolate himself, deflate his people, and push his best team members out the door, then congratulations, this leader did a fantastic job. But somehow, I don't think that was his intention.

If you really want to gain an edge as a leader, you have to think about truly effective ways of motivating people—by which I mean over the long term, not just short-term scare tactics. If you have high expectations for people (like we talked about in the last chapter), which means you are putting a lot of pressure on them, you need to balance that by finding positive and inspiring ways to motivate them.

I think back to Bernardo Hees and what he said to me when I was offered the position at Burger King. When he said he would fire me in six months if I didn't turn the business around, it wasn't a threat; it was a challenge. It was also critical information. He was telling me what was expected of me, what I needed to do to succeed. He talked about how I would be *rewarded* when I *succeeded*. That is a whole lot different from threatening to fire someone if he/she voices a complaint or has concerns about roles or expectations.

The difference goes back to two things: intention and follow-through. If Hees hadn't supported me in my efforts to fulfill his expectations or if telling me he was going to fire me became a repeated behavior, something he said every time we disagreed or he wanted to put pressure on me, then I would have reacted very differently over time. I would have gotten tired of working under threat and gone elsewhere. But that is not what happened. Instead, he championed my plans to turn around the business and rewarded my success when I did, just as he promised he would.

A better way for that tech company executive to address the problem he was facing would have been to say something like this: "I understand that there are a lot of questions and concerns about what's going to happen now that we are under new ownership. To be completely honest with you, no one has all the answers at the present moment. This is a new situation for all of us and we are still figuring things out. I can't give you all the answers right now, but I can promise to continue to keep you all informed. In the meantime, I need your help in making this transition as smooth as possible and keeping the focus on meeting our new objectives."

There is something truly motivating about making people feel like you are on the same side and asking for their help. The latter puts them in an empowered position rather than a disempowered one—which is how people feel when they are being threatened. If you want to set high expectations, you need people to feel empowered, not beaten down, in order to deliver on those expectation.

Inspiring Leaders Help People Dream Big

What can leaders do to motivate people? The opposite of leading by intimidation is leading by inspiration. In a nutshell, that is what the phrase *Dream big* means in this context. It means inspiring people to dream big about what they can do, what they can become, and how they can contribute to something bigger than themselves. It means helping them to lead happy, healthy, supported, and productive lives so they can be the best they can be and do the best work they can do for your company.

In order to do this, you have to ask yourself a couple of questions:

- How can the organization help support the goals of my team members?

- How can I help support the goals of my team members?

This goes back to the first section in this book, where I talked about getting to know people and what they care about. Every person's dreams are going to be different. One person might want to be CEO one day, while another might just be looking to provide a good and stable life for her family. Someone else might be looking for a sense of purpose in his daily life while another might have education goals in mind. The more you know about what makes someone tick, the more you can help that person grow and take steps toward fulfilling his or her dreams.

Why is this so important? When people are learning, growing, and expanding their capabilities, the company will benefit. These are the best conditions for people to work hard, come up with new innovations, and take on new roles and responsibilities. Team members will feel more invested in the company's success when they feel that their dreams, goals, and values intersect with those of the company.

Leading by Inspiration

No one likes to go to work day in, day out, feeling like they are doing little more than bringing home a paycheck. That's not inspiring. That's not motivating. Leaders can help people to

- Pursue their dreams

- Feel heard, supported, and cared about

- Feel that their lives are in balance

- Enjoy what they do and where they work

- Feel part of something bigger than themselves

These are the kinds of motivations that give people, and the organization they work for, a leading edge.

Inspiring Leaders Show People They Care

When I was growing up, my father taught me an important lesson about leadership: People perform better when they care about what they're doing. It's a simple idea, but it's also an idea that tends to get overlooked. Many managers think, I pay these people; isn't that enough? Well, have you ever phoned in sick at work or known someone who has? That person was still getting paid, right? Money alone is not enough to truly motivate people.

A simple but highly effective way leaders can help people care more about the business is to show that you care about them. Show them that you feel as invested in them as you want them to be in the business. After all, how can you expect people to care about the company when they don't feel that the company or its leaders care about them?

This goes beyond caring about their work and how well they are doing it. It means caring about them as human beings who have lives outside the office. There are a number of ways that you can show people that you care about them. The following are a few ways to get you started:

1) *Ask people about themselves*: Find out about people's spouses and kids. Learn about their hobbies and interests. This is simple get-to-know-you stuff, but just because it's simple, doesn't mean it isn't valuable. In today's fast-paced world, people too often overlook the basics of establishing solid relationships. Don't make that mistake no matter how busy you are. After all, you are not just leading roles or leading job functions; you are leading *people* and people have lives outside the office.

2) *Show your appreciation*: As leaders, we often have to put pressure on people to get things done. You can balance that by also making a point of showing your thanks for how much effort someone is putting in or how much extra time they have spent on a project. Bring doughnuts and coffee the next time team members are in the office early to work on a special project. Or give someone an extra day off after they have completed a time-consuming task. Even taking the

time to say to someone "I know how hard you worked on this and I wanted to say thank you" can go a long way.

3) *Notice changes in people's moods or behaviors*: At Young and Rubicam, we brought in an interim CFO after our previous one had left abruptly. It was a difficult time for the company, and we really needed this guy to help us keep the lights on while we did a thorough executive search for a permanent replacement. Our interim CFO knew this and that was why he felt so conflicted when he found out his wife was facing a new cancer diagnosis. He wanted to be with his family, but he also took the commitment he had made to the company very seriously.

He didn't say much about his situation, but I could see that something was gnawing at him. He was quieter than usual and often seemed distracted, so I pulled him aside and asked if anything was wrong. His concern about his wife just spilled out. I immediately suggested he forget about everything in the office for a while and be with his family. I think he really needed someone to tell him it was okay to take care of himself and his family first.

Besides being the right thing to do, that simple act of caring paid off. Everything worked out with the interim CFO's wife, and when he returned to work, he was more focused than ever. As an added benefit, the rest of the finance department really rallied together to cover for him while he was away. Others find caring about someone and helping them through difficult circumstances to be motivating too.

Looking for Clues

How do you pick up on people's moods so you know when they might need a little extra caring? Here are some clues about what to look for:

- Body language: A person's body language will often tell you a lot about what's not being said aloud. If you see someone walking with his head down or sitting alone at lunch when he is usually quite social, take note. Or maybe someone has a spring in her step or a big smile on her face. Any changes in how people carry themselves are worth asking about. You obviously don't want to be intrusive, but a simple "You seem different today—is something going on?" generally works well. If the person doesn't want to talk about it, then you have to respect that, but usually you will get some sort of answer. Regardless of whether you gain additional insight or not, you have still shown the person that you care.

- Energy level and engagement: When someone appears less talkative in meetings or more withdrawn, it's an indication that it's time to pay closer attention. I was once having lunch with a sales associate when I noticed he was a lot less chatty than usual. After making several attempts to drive the conversation and getting only minimal participation, I switched from talking about the business to talking about him. "I don't feel the same level of energy from you today that I'm used to," I said. "Is everything okay?" After that he started opening up. We had had three people resign in the previous week, and he was upset by it. He didn't know why they had left—two had been for personal reasons, the other because he was in danger of being fired for poor performance—and he felt uncomfortable about it.

> He wondered if they had been pressured out and if the same might happen to him. I told him a little about why the people had gone and reassured him that his job wasn't in jeopardy. After that, he perked up almost immediately.

Inspiring Leaders Promote Work-life Balance

A highly effective way to show people you care—particularly in this day and age—is by helping them strike a healthy work-life balance. This is another key lesson I learned from my father. He taught me that balance isn't just important for one's personal well-being; it's a crucial part of excelling in every aspect of life. He was a very successful entrepreneur who built his business from nothing. In order to do that, he naturally had to work long hours and travel a lot. You might think he sacrificed time with his family as a result, but he didn't. Every time he went on a business trip, he brought my mother along with him. No matter what was going on at work, he always made it home for dinner with his family, every single night. Rather than keeping his work and home lives separate, he often brought his family to work. I remember running around his office when I was four or five years old.

So many of us seem to believe that we can put work in one box, our families in another, our own personal satisfaction in yet another. People talk about how technology is breaching those walls, bringing work into our home lives and vice versa. Well, I don't believe those walls were ever really there. Take a simple example: One morning you wake up and walk into the kitchen. Your spouse is giving the kids breakfast. As you pour yourself some coffee, he or she reminds you of the dinner you have planned that night with friends. "Shoot, I forgot," you say. "Do you think we could put it off until next week? It's going to be a long day at the office."

That kicks off an argument. Then one of the kids starts crying because he doesn't like when his parents fight. The two of you hash it out, but you have to leave for work before you can come to a real resolution. You have an early meeting and you can't be late.

How effective do you think you are going to be at that meeting? If you are really honest with yourself, can you truly say that you will be as good, or better, than you would have been if you hadn't gotten into an argument that morning?

It will take extra effort and concentration to move past that morning's argument and make good decisions that are unaffected by the emotions it brought up. And that's just the effect of one argument. Imagine the effect a bad relationship has on your career, or conversely, the effect a job you hate has on your personal life. On some level, we all know it's true: We only have one life to live. The real secret that my dad taught me is that when we succeed in one aspect of our lives, we are all the more likely to succeed in all of them. Whatever is happening in your personal life can never be left entirely at home. It affects how you work and it affects how you feel at work, how motivated you are, maybe even how much time you can spend on something.

Take the example I gave before about our interim CFO who was worried about his wife. It was constantly on his mind, so of course it affected how he performed. It would for anyone. You can help someone in a situation like that by giving them the time they need to work through the issue. Even letting them vent or talk something through is going to make him or her more effective in the long run. When people feel better about what is happening at home, they will be that much more invested and focused when they are at work.

Effective Ways of Improving Work-life Balance

There are countless ways that leaders can help people balance the different areas of their lives and the various pressures put on them as a result. Here are a few ways to consider, and you can look for additional ways that will make the most difference to the people you lead:

1) *Flexible schedules*: When I was at Yum! Brands, we were offered summer hours and holiday hours; we could choose to come to the office an hour earlier and leave an hour later Monday through Thursday so that we could take off Friday afternoons to be with our families during those times when kids were out of school. People really appreciated having that choice even though they typically ended up working more hours during the week, not less, albeit on a different timetable. Nonetheless, if they chose to do it, they did it happily, and that is the key to motivation. You can also be flexible about letting team members work from home when a child is sick, come in early so they can leave early a couple of days a week in order to take a class. There are any number of ways that time can be used to help people pursue their dreams or restore themselves.

2) *Make it a family affair*: Help people to better integrate their work and personal lives by making the workplace family-friendly. No matter how much his company grew, my father never lost his family approach to leadership. Every Christmas he would host a holiday party for the entire company and their families. He always worked hard to ensure that it was a memorable event for everyone's children by buying presents for every child under the age of twelve and hiring a Santa Claus to give them out. He would also sponsor sports teams for his employee's kids (and give his employees time off to coach the teams—another example of the first tactic). It didn't matter if it was a

receptionist or a vice president, he would always send flowers, balloons, and a gift to the hospital to say congratulations when someone had a new baby. The family-friendly spirit he was able to bring to his company was really motivating. When you feel like family, it's harder to let each other down.

3) *Healthy lifestyle*: I wake up at five most mornings so I can work out before going to the office. That is my personal time to recharge. It's good for my energy level and overall health, and it just makes me feel better throughout the day. The modern-day workplace, with so many of us sitting for long hours in front of computer screens, is not always conducive to physical health, but it doesn't have to be that way. From discounts on gym memberships to company softball teams, there are many ways that leaders can help team members lead healthier lives.

4) *Listen to people's needs*: A big reason why people leave a job is because something about it doesn't fit with the lifestyle they want to lead. Maybe the hours make it difficult to put their kids to bed at night. Maybe the commute is too long and stressful. You can't fix everything for people, but it's always worth asking if there is something you can do to make things easier, especially for your top performers. I remember hearing John Donahoe, the former CEO of eBay, talk about a time earlier in his career when all the travel he was doing was making it difficult for him to balance his work and home life. To show how much the company valued John, his boss offered him a creative solution: They found a client near where Donahoe lived that he could focus on exclusively, which allowed him to spend more time with his family, even drop his kids off at school in the mornings. By taking the time to understand where Donahoe was coming from, his boss was able to remove some of the barriers that were getting in the way of him working at his optimum level. The

result, as Donahoe described it was "the most productive year of my career."

Inspiring Leaders Create Fun, Shared Experiences

Another way of motivating people is by creating fun, shared experiences. These kinds of experiences help individuals feel more invested in their fellow team members by encouraging them to spend time with one another and let off steam together. They also make the workplace a more enjoyable place to be. It's simple: People work harder and do a better job when they like what they do and where they do it.

At Burger King, we implemented a yearly marketing meeting where we would bring marketing staff from thirty-two countries together at some appealing destination. We would spend a couple of days together, talking through strategy and action plans for the following calendar year, and we would take the opportunity to create a lot of fun, team-building activities. One of the most memorable for me was when about fifty of us went kayaking at night through the mangroves of Puerto Rico. It was a bonding experience that people talked about for years afterward. The following year we went to Mexico City, then to Medellín, Colombia, the year after that. There is something about getting people together in a new environment that helps them open up and become more creative. I think that was a large part of what made us so successful at Burger King. We had a solid team of people who liked each other and trusted one another. These shared experiences played a big part in laying that foundation.

Of course, you don't have to leave the office to have a little fun. You can throw parties to celebrate reaching a big goal or gaining a new client. At Driven Brands, we had "beer Fridays" where everyone would get together over a drink to hang out and blow off steam. One day, I hired an ice cream truck to park in the lot of our corporate office and invited everyone to enjoy free ice cream. It was my way of saying thank you for all their hard work. The possibilities are endless. Just use your imagination and make a point of bringing a little fun into people's workdays.

Inspiring Leaders Make People Feel Part of Something Bigger

During my first ninety days at Maaco, I went on that listening tour that I described earlier. I sat down with as many franchisees as I could and used the insights I gathered to help craft a vision for where the business could go. But I didn't stop there. I then took that vision back to the franchisees so they could contribute their input. This process worked out incredibly well because it made everyone feel that they were contributing, helping to figure out what our shared future would look like and how we would get there.

It's pretty easy for employees to get tunnel vision, especially in larger companies. A lot of your team members may know what they are required to do, but not how their piece of the puzzle fits with all the other pieces in all the other departments throughout the organization. This can leave people feeling isolated and uninspired. Knowing what you need to do is not the same as knowing why you are doing it.

I think everyone wants to feel that they are part of something larger than themselves. They also want to know how they fit into that bigger picture. Do they matter? How do their contributions affect others, affect the whole? It's motivating to know that you can make a difference. When you are setting big goals for people, when you are providing them with feedback on how they are performing, make sure that those conversations include some insight on how their goals and accomplishments are contributing to the bigger picture.

All of the Above... with Authenticity

Not long after I got married, a coworker came into my office to ask me for some help on something. "So how is Cindy?" he asked, without much feeling. I started to answer but cut it short when it became clear that he wasn't really listening. As soon as I paused, he immediately jumped in to ask his favor, not even acknowledging what I had said about my wife. It was clear to me that he didn't really care. He just felt like he should try to be polite before asking for my help.

It was such an off-putting experience that I still remember it all these years later. And that is a critical thing to keep in mind. You can use all the advice and tactics I have laid out in this chapter, but they won't really work if your efforts don't come across as authentic to the people you are trying to motivate.

The person who asked me about my wife was single, so maybe he wasn't that interested in talking about marriage. That's okay, even understandable, but surely he could have found some other way to connect. The point is that if you start to make a list of the people you find inspiring in the world today (see my list in the sidebar for some ideas), you will quickly realize that people can inspire you for different reasons. You don't have to be someone you're not to motivate people. You don't have to be a certain kind of person. There are different ways to motivate, and you should find what works for you, what fits with your style and your personality, and what best suits the organization you are part of. That is the best way for your efforts to feel authentic.

In order to do this, make use of that self-awareness I talked about in the first section. Know your strengths and think about how you can use them to engage and connect. So many of the things I have talked about in this chapter don't have to cost a lot or even take all that much time or effort on your part. Simple, authentic gestures are often the most effective, so why not use them to inspire your people and motivate them to do bigger and better things?

Leaders Who Have Inspired Me

There are so many different ways that leaders can inspire people. Following is a list of people who have inspired me, all of whom have different styles and distinct personalities.

David Novak: When I was at Yum! Brands, Novak was the chairman and CEO. He was a very engaging, personable guy with a lot of energy and an optimistic outlook. He reminded me of a football coach in the energetic way he would rally people. In fact, he always preferred the word *coach* instead of *boss* because he believed that was a better, more productive, more inspiring way of characterizing the relationship between people and their supervisors. After any team meeting with Novak, it literally felt like you had just left the huddle, the play had been called, and you were ready to go lead your team to victory. He was and is a true motivator.

Bernardo Hees: Hees was the CEO of Burger King when I worked there. He was a tough, no-nonsense leader who would often use silence to drive a point home. He would ask someone a direct question like "Why aren't these sales figures as high as we had projected" and then just look you in the eyes and wait for your response—your full response, even if you fumbled your answer. That was always very motivating because you felt that he really expected you to succeed, or at least have a good well-thought-out answer when you didn't.

Chip Edens: The rector at my church in Charlotte has always been inspiring to me for his ability to connect with just about anyone. He comes across as very open and approachable right away, which makes him easy to talk to. I have seen him speak easily with a person he just met, and I have seen him do it in front of a crowd of thousands. He truly cares about people and that feeling comes through when he talks to them.

LeBron James: When I watch James on TV, he always seems to be able to get people fired up in any circumstances. Whether his team is ahead or behind, he has this ability to rally the people around him. Every time he changes teams, his new team does well even if it only had mediocre results before. I think that's because he makes people feel that they can succeed, even if they are not the best players on the team. That is a skill that goes beyond being a great athlete.

Malala Yousafzai: Inspired me because she was able to turn a tragic experience, being brutally attacked by a terrorist group, into a platform to advocate for education among young women. At 17 years of age she received the Nobel Prize and is now on a mission to change the world through social activism. Today she's only 21 years old and she's one of the best female leaders I've ever seen.

6: Work Hard—Reward Results and Promote Meritocracy

Being the kind of leader who inspires people to dream big doesn't mean you aren't also results-driven. Too often people feel that these ideas are in conflict, but they really aren't at all. Caring about people and caring about the bottom line are not mutually exclusive. In fact, when you avoid being honest with people about their lack of abilities or poor performance, it puts them in an awkward position. They may feel a lack of respect and appreciation from those around them but not fully understand why. In addition, it leaves them open to an unpleasant surprise if they are managed out without sufficient warning.

Big dreams and hard work are perfect complements to one another. After all, dreams mean very little if a person doesn't do what it takes to realize them. That is where hard work comes in, and leaders can do a lot to foster an environment in which a high value is placed on hard work. The best way to ensure that those big dreams are backed up by hard work is to reward the results you want and make meritocracy a driving force in your workplace culture. This chapter is about how to pay people back for working hard toward those big dreams and what to do about those who are missing the mark.

Recognize Hard Work

Recognition is about noticing when someone is excelling in some important way and calling attention to that fact with accolades and rewards. It's an important tool for leaders to use because everyone wants to feel important and appreciated for what they do. It's something that practically all of us are hardwired to respond to since we were kids. We all grew up with recognition at school in the form of grades, in sports with trophies and ribbons, in the Boy or Girl Scouts with badges. Our good work was rewarded, and there is no reason why that same principle shouldn't extend to the workplace.

My first exposure to recognition in a corporate setting was at Yum! Brands, where I took a job right out of graduate school. The CEO at the time, David Novak, really championed the idea and made it a big part of the company's culture in all its locations around the world. Every leader in the organization came up with his or her own award to recognize hard work and extraordinary results among their team members. There was a whole range of whimsical and memorable awards from boxing gloves to golden shovels. At one point I was responsible for managing the relationship between KFC and one of our primary vendors, Pepsi. To recognize me for doing such a good job of handling that account, my boss presented me with a beverage helmet—a kind of baseball helmet with two Pepsi cans on top attached to a drinking tube. The awards, which were given out publicly and often in Yum! Brand offices, were always fun and made a lasting impression.

The program was so effective I stole the idea. When I started my own advertising agency, COSTA IMC, I created an employee recognition program. I did the same at Burger King and then again at GrandVision, where it was something completely new among the members of our management team. I have spent years publicly recognizing employees at quarterly all-employee meetings, even when other senior leaders didn't join in or support the program. It has been a lesson in conviction because I could have shied away when I saw that others weren't following my lead, but I persisted because I think recognition is that important. At one company I worked for, I recognized people for several years before another executive finally started giving out his own awards. To my surprise, he gave his very first one to me for inspiring him and showing him the value of recognition.

As with anything else, recognition needs to be done right for it to have a meaningful impact. I will talk more about the whens and hows in the coming sections. First I want to spend some time highlighting why it's such an effective tool for leaders to use. It starts with motivation. We spent the last chapter talking about the importance of motivating people, but a leader can easily undo that motivational spirit by not recognizing or appreciating hard work. After all, who wants to work really hard only to have their efforts go unnoticed? Recent research by the UBC Sauder School of Business at the University of British Columbia in Vancouver, Canada, suggests that paying no attention is even more damaging to employees' sense of well-being and engagement than negative attention ("Is Negative Attention Better Than No Attention?" *Organization Science*, April 4, 2014). It's not all that surprising if you think about it. No one likes to be ignored, so a little attention—especially positive attention—paid to the right things can really make a big difference.

Recognition also reinforces those high expectations we have already talked about by helping to build a culture of meritocracy—a person gets acknowledged and rewarded *only after* fulfilling those expectations. If you have been setting clear goals and expectations, then you can use those to measure people's progress in a fair and transparent way and recognize real success. That is important for the individual being recognized, and it's also important for everyone else because it conveys a message about what it takes to get ahead.

Recognition is a tool that doesn't have to cost a lot in terms of time, effort, or money but can nonetheless make a big impact. At COSTA IMC, we used recognition to help us through a tough situation after our Vice President of Finance left abruptly. We were in the process of changing the "plumbing" of the entire department—the people, systems, and technology—in order to grow more when the Vice President left without notice. Over the course of the next three months, several consulting firms were brought in and five more top leaders on the finance team either resigned or were fired. To put it bluntly, the entire department was a mess. The team members who remained were left feeling unhappy, unmotivated, and completely unsettled.

As a result, I started a recognition program for the finance department to call attention to those who were going above and beyond to help us through this difficult transitional time. Along with some other senior leaders, I did "lunch-and-learns," where members of the executive team took key staff members to lunch in order to invite questions, provide them with personal coaching, and let them know how important their contributions were to us and to the company. We recognized many of them publicly as well by giving out awards and bonuses. About eight critical people in the department rose to the occasion and really helped us through until we found a new Vice President. Everything worked out in the end, but the situation could have been a disaster if we hadn't used recognition to inspire people to work hard and feel invested in the company during the toughest of circumstances, when they had every reason to abandon ship.

When to Recognize

The short answer is *as often as possible*. By recognizing people often and publicly for their accomplishments, leaders have a powerful tool for sending a message about which results and behaviors matter most to them. Recognition can be done at two different times: on a regular basis, when people are expecting it, and in the moment or spontaneously, when people aren't expecting it. Both are valuable in different ways and should be used liberally by leaders looking for an edge:

- *Monthly and/or quarterly formal recognition*: By this I mean awards given out on a regular basis so that people come to expect them. At GrandVision, I give out two awards at every quarterly all-employee meeting in front of the entire company starting with the first quarterly meeting I ever participated in. I do the same thing on a smaller scale at monthly staff meetings. I make a point of doing this at every single meeting so that people know it's coming. That expectation gives them something to work toward as they're pursing their own big dreams and those of the company.

- *In-the-moment, informal recognition*: As with giving formal feedback to people, recognition can be done spontaneously too, any time you catch someone doing something that merits a special thank you. Every week I make a point of looking for opportunities to do this, like when I see a team member volunteering to help someone who is on a tight deadline or when I see someone go the extra mile for a customer. With this kind of informal recognition, you don't reach the entire company like you do when you publicly recognize someone at a meeting. However, you do get to convey to people, one on one, that you see and appreciate them, which is motivating and fosters a sense of loyalty. You also get to tie recognition to very specific actions that you want to see more of.

How to Recognize People's Achievements

There are different ways for leaders to recognize people's achievements. Following is a look at three of the most common, all of which can be effective when used to emphasize and reward results that matter to you and to the organization:

1) *Awards*: The ubiquitous Employee of the Month plaque or certificate is what first comes to mind for many people when they think about recognition awards. I learned at Yum! Brands, however, that they can be much more creative, memorable, and therefore effective than that. During our quarterly all-employee meetings at Driven Brands, I chose to give out huge rubber duckies as my awards —the kind kids play with in the bathtub, only supersized. I gave them to those team members who had shown the ability "to swim beyond where they were expected to go" by delivering more than what had been asked of them. Before that I gave out model cars: a red car for Carstar, a blue one for Maaco, and a green car for Drive N Style. At one point I even gave out *Game of Thrones* figurines to people who had shown special skills and a fighting spirit.

Every time I walked into our conference room with a huge rubber ducky under my arm, people would smile because it added a bit of fun to the proceedings. Everyone came to know that this meant I was going to recognize someone. When I did, I would stand front and center and do it publicly, making a big point of explaining why the person was getting the award. I would start, not by saying the person's name, but by explaining the accomplishments that had merited the award. I would say something like: "This is for a person who went above and beyond, delivering three reports well ahead of time about whether we should or should not acquire a new company. Her analysis was invaluable in helping us make that critical decision..."

The person being recognized would pick up on the fact that he or she was being honored by my description, but many others wouldn't know whom I was talking about. To add a bit of drama, I wouldn't reveal the name until the very end. Then I would call the person to the front of the conference room to get the award. In addition to the rubber ducky, I would include a personal note of thanks that detailed what the award was for.

Those awards became conversation starters because people would display them on their desks or in their cubicles. When someone saw a rubber ducky on a colleague's desk, they were almost sure to ask about it. Who wouldn't? The same happened with suppliers and visitors who would want to know what it was and why it was there. That gave recipients an opportunity to talk about their accomplishments with pride. It also reinforced what we valued as an organization because people would talk about *why* they had deserved to be recognized — spreading the word to others about what it took to stand out.

I think the choice of award is key: You notice a rubber ducky, whereas you may not notice a certificate on somebody's wall. It helps make the office space fun, which is one of the motivational tactics I talked about in the last chapter. Your choice also says something about you as a leader, making it more personal than just some cash (not that cash should be discounted) or a plaque. Recognition works best when it's personal, memorable, and fun.

2) *Thank-yous*: For more informal, spontaneous recognition. I often leave a thank-you note with a gift card for a local restaurant or coffee shop on someone's desk. Again, I always make explicit in the note what I'm thanking the person for. Sometimes I will do something a bit more personal, especially if it's someone I know well or work with often. My assistant helps me with so many things that I will often get her flowers or her favorite chocolates. If someone comes in early to work on a project for me, I will go on a Starbucks run to show my appreciation. If team members are working through lunch on a tight deadline, I will order in food or treat them to lunch once they have finished. If someone puts in a lot of extra time on something, I might say thank you with an extra vacation day.

In my view, small gestures like these are underutilized by leaders. They are so easy to do and can have such a big effect. They breed trust and loyalty. They help build a culture of civility and appreciation for one another's contributions. They show people that you actively care about results and the kinds of behaviors that lead to them. They show that you are watching and aware of what they do. These things are not to be underestimated. Even a simple verbal *thank you* can make all the difference in someone's day.

3) *Monetary rewards*: Finally, there is the most expected way of recognizing someone — monetary rewards, either in the form of raises or bonuses. Expected though they might be, these still need to be doled out strategically. The second year I was at Driven Brands, we (the management team) decided to give a bonus of $1,000 to two employees each quarter based on a company-wide vote. A thousand dollars is a lot of money to surprise someone with, so it really made an impact on the recipient. By the way, these bonuses were completely separate from the quarterly rubber ducky awards that I talked about before (which, I should mention, also included $100 in cash just to make them that much more valuable to the recipient).

When I was on the CBS show *Undercover Boss*, I gave away monetary amounts that were truly life-changing. For those team members who had really shown themselves to be hard workers and who taught me so much about our front-line business, I gave anywhere from $50,000 to $60,000 per person, which was used for things like a college fund for one person's kids, a down payment on a first home for another, and buying a car to provide an easier commute to work for yet another. These were examples of how money can have a big emotional impact on people when it makes a real, positive difference in their lives and helps them fulfill their dreams.

What to Recognize

When you recognize someone, you need to make sure the recognition is clearly tied to performance. When I give out my big recognition awards at all-employee meetings, for example, it's always to someone who has gone above and beyond what has been asked of them — someone who took on extra responsibility, put in extra hours to hit a tough benchmark, or came up with a new innovation. It can also be for someone who delivers top results time and time again. Consistency like that is definitely worth rewarding in a big way.

Recognition can also be a great way to reinforce the values a company wants to promote. For example, we have five values at GrandVision, and each quarter we recognize someone who exemplifies one of those values. One quarter we might recognize a person for *making bold moves* because that's one of our values. That could be for a person who came up with a process innovation or who signed a big new client who had previously remained elusive. The next quarter the award might be given for living up to our value of *accountability*. That could go to someone who has taken on extra responsibility or who has stepped in to put out a metaphoric fire amid a crisis.

In the speech that accompanies the award presentation, that value is then articulated and examples are given of how the recipient has exemplified and excelled at it. In this way, you emphasize the results and behaviors you want while reinforcing the company culture you are trying to build.

Recognition Gone Wrong

Recognition can certainly be done badly, in a way that is demoralizing or sends the wrong signals to people about what is important to you and the organization. It can't just be about the numbers. It's easy to look at your sales figures and pick out the salesperson who is on top that month. That person could obviously be a candidate for an award, but you also have to look at how they got those results. You have to look at how that person interacts with other members of the team, contributes to the culture, and supports the values you are trying to promote in the company.

If you are publicly recognizing someone who doesn't exemplify the behaviors and values of the company, then it can really backfire. I once worked with a salesman who made great numbers, but he also made a lot of people uncomfortable. He traveled a lot, and it was well known that, even though he often closed deals during the day, he spent a lot of evenings in the hotel bar drinking too much and picking up women. (Did I mention the guy was married?) After a while, it came to our attention that this salesman had sexually harassed someone in his department. We fired him on the spot. Can you imagine what sort of message it would have sent to his coworkers if he had been publicly recognized for his sales results?

By the same token, the old tradition of honoring someone who has stuck around for a number of years should be abandoned. It doesn't matter how long someone has been with the company; it matters how they have performed during that time. You never want to recognize people just because they have reached some anniversary date on the calendar or because they haven't been given an award yet and think it's their turn. Recognition should always be 100 percent about merit, about specific accomplishments that you can point to and brag about. That is for the benefit of the receiver and for everyone else.

A Culture of Meritocracy

Establishing a meritocracy means creating an environment where performance is what matters most. It means making it clear, through words and actions, that anyone can get ahead by achieving their goals, exceeding expectations, and contributing in a positive way to the company's culture, values, or bottom line. This is one of the main purposes behind recognition — to celebrate and promote those very ideals and the people who embody them.

One of the secrets to creating this kind of culture is to make everything as objective and transparent as possible. If you assign everyone a scorecard at the beginning of the year, then they will know what is expected of them. If you then do many of the things that we have already talked about — track their progress, make their results clear and public, and check in with them on a regular basis to provide feedback and guidance — then it should be obvious at all times how well each person is performing. Remember the lesson of the last section: We aim for an atmosphere of no surprises. If we do this successfully, individuals will not be caught off guard, and the organization won't be caught off guard by the poor performance of a few individuals. If things start to stray off course, away from stated objectives, then we can help a person to pivot or adjust. And the people who outperform those objectives are the ones who get recognized and promoted. It all comes together to send a consistent message. Whether you are talking about recognition or rewards, or a person's pay or title, everything needs to align at all times with the goals and values you are trying to further as a company.

Another secret to building a meritocracy is fairness or balance. If you want people to know you have high expectations, you have to have them for everyone. If you have certain results and behaviors that you use as a yardstick, they need to be applied evenly across the board. Letting something slide with one employee who is well-intentioned but has fallen below the mark may seem empathetic at the time, but you have to weigh that against the effect it has on others. Letting something slide for one person may make the job more difficult for someone else or for the team as a whole. It may also serve to discourage people; after all, why work so hard if failure doesn't have consequences?

How to Recognize Bad Results

Promoting meritocracy means recognizing the bad as well as the good. I prefer to emphasize the positive, but that doesn't mean I won't call out people who have made mistakes or who aren't living up to expectations. Criticizing someone's work or calling attention to poor results is never fun or comfortable. The person on the receiving end is certainly not going to enjoy it, but neither will most leaders who have to deliver unwelcome news. There are, however, ways of handling bad results that are far more productive than others.

First you have to determine whether someone has had an isolated bad outcome or whether that outcome is part of an unfortunate pattern. If someone has made a single mistake, the best thing you can do is be honest and direct. Point out the problem, be clear about why it's a problem, and then let the person offer an explanation. For example, I once promoted someone, transferring her to a different division in the process. She was thrilled, but the news changed the way she treated the colleagues she would soon be leaving behind. She still had a few weeks to go in her old position before the promotion took effect, and during that time she stopped playing nice with others. I guess she figured that since she wouldn't be working with those people much longer, it would be okay to be rude to and dismissive of them.

Word came back to me about this during my one-on-one meetings with people. I wasn't just hearing it from her direct reports but from her peers and even her supervisors. So I collected all this feedback and presented it to her in our next one-on-one. I let her digest it and then I said to her, "If you want to continue to grow within the organization, you cannot behave this way under any circumstances. We need team players around here and even though these people will no longer be part of your team, the way you treated them doesn't speak well for you or your ability to build strong relationships with members of the new team you are about to join, or any team you become part of in the future."

To her credit, she got it immediately. She admitted that her promotion had gone to her head and that she had been so focused on moving on that she hadn't given any thought to walking out the division door with grace. She apologized to me and then to the team members she had offended. We left it at that. For a while, I paid extra attention to reports of her behavior from her new team members, but all indications were that she had learned her lesson.

Once you are sure that a point has been made, I believe it's important to let things go so people don't feel berated over their failings. No one likes to be reminded of their worst moments, especially if they have worked to move past them. Of course, this assumes that people don't continue to fail to live up to expectations. If they do, that needs to be recognized too.

The Importance of Letting People Go

Unfortunately, building a meritocracy also means that at some point you are going to have to let people go. Getting rid of underperformers is necessary because it sends a message to everyone who remains that their hard work matters and that a lack of hard work and results won't be tolerated.

At GrandVision, we track results regularly, and we rank everyone in the company twice a year. We used that nine-box matrix that I covered in chapter 2, and everyone knows if they receive two reviews where they land in the bottom left-hand corner of the matrix—the Low Potential/Low Performance box—then they are going to have to exit the organization.

Because of our open-concept office, people will notice when someone is suddenly gone. But because we are so public with our results, with every employee knowing all of our metrics across board—operational, financial, sales, customer satisfaction, etc.—when someone is let go, it rarely comes as a surprise, to that person or to anyone else.

The flip side is that if it had been obvious to all that someone was at the bottom of the rankings for several quarters and we didn't do anything about it, then we would have lost credibility as leaders. Growing up in the advertising agency world, I saw multiple examples of companies that were pretty complacent about poor performers. There were employees who probably shouldn't have been there, and it had a ripple effect. It didn't bring down the company, but it did lower standards across the board and affected people's investment and motivation.

Of course, there are situations where firing someone does come as a surprise. If someone does something that simply cannot be tolerated—like the employee I mentioned before who sexually harassed a colleague—then you have to deal with it quickly and decisively.

There is no room for warnings. In situations like that, where questions may arise from the rest of the staff about what happens, it's still best to be as open and transparent as possible (even if you don't tell people the full story) for the sake of fostering that meritocracy that is so important. In any organization there are going to be individuals who believe that someone got promoted or let go for personal or political reasons that are unfair and have nothing to do with merit. The best thing you can do is return to the objective data, making it as plain and available as possible. At that point, if people don't understand why something happened, it's because they choose not to.

How to Let Someone Go with Grace

Early in my career, I witnessed a stark example of how not to let someone go, which has stuck with me ever since. This man was older, probably in his sixties, and he had been with the company forever—practically his entire adult life. In fact, it was more than that. He had started with the company when he was just fifteen years old. After something like forty-five years or more with the company, he was nearing retirement when one day a manager walked in, sat down next to him in the middle of our open-concept office, and told him that it was his last day on the job. The manager did this in front of everyone, not even bothering to lower his voice so people wouldn't overhear. Afterward, the man who had been fired started crying. I will never forget how badly I felt watching that happen while people went about their business all around him.

That man may have been gone the next day, but you better believe that everyone who stayed noticed and talked about the way he was let go. The manager cast an unbelievably bad shadow. The manager's actions contributed to a serious lack of trust in management and a feeling that the company didn't really value its people as it claimed to.

Leaders had to grapple with the fallout from that day—which was really just a symptom of larger cultural problems—for a long time to come.

Meritocracy means having some tough conversations from time to time, but that never means you have to set aside your humanity in the process. The best example I have ever seen of firing someone with grace was demonstrated by my boss at Burger King, Jose Tomas, who went on to become the chief people officer for General Motors. He had the unenviable task of letting people go on a semi-regular basis, and I sat with him in the conference room on a number of occasions while he did it. It was an incredible thing to witness. It was like watching someone break up with a boyfriend or girlfriend in high school, using the old standby "It's not you, it's me" approach, only people tended to believe him. Nine times out of ten the person would walk out of the room, having just been let go, but with a fairly positive attitude.

I once asked Jose how he did it, and he explained that after many years in HR, he had learned a few key things:

1. *You don't have to be a jerk.* Just because it's an unpleasant experience to have to tell someone they are fired doesn't mean you should take it out on that person. Go in there with as much empathy as you can muster. Then get to the point quickly—there is no reason to drag out the discomfort for either of you.

2. *Let the person save face.* Honesty is incredibly important to me, but Jose taught me that in a situation where the person is already on the way out the door, brutal honesty is unnecessary and maybe even cruel. He would say something like "Your position is being eliminated," "We've made the decision to part ways," or "We feel there is not a great

match for you within the organization anymore" rather than spend time dwelling on the person's failures. Burger King was a merit-based organization, so people usually knew the deal without needing it rubbed it in their faces.

3. *Offer to help.* After telling someone they were being let go, Jose typically followed up quickly with an olive branch. He might say, "John, this is an uncomfortable conversation. You're being terminated, but I want to help you out." Then he would offer something specific: "I'm always willing to help if you want to connect with recruiters or need any references." This let people know that they weren't just being cut off, which was a kind of comfort in a difficult situation.

4. *Play with incentives.* Jose would always look for the proverbial spoonful of sugar that could make the HR medicine go down easier. He might offer a generous severance. He once said to someone, "I noticed you are two months away from your 401(k) vesting. I have talked to my supervisor, and we are able to make sure that still happens even though you are leaving early." It's not always possible to offer something like that, but if you get to know a bit about the person first, you might come up with something that will help. After all, losing a job is scary and stressful, so even little things can make a difference.

People would often walk out of those meetings with Jose feeling as though it was the beginning of something new for them, not the end. That was truly a gift. I was grateful for his lessons when, after opening my own agency in 2007, the recession hit just a year later and I had to fire sixteen people. I sat down with each person, one on one, and explained the circumstances, letting them all know that it wasn't their fault. I had letters of recommendation already written to give to them. I offered to do whatever I could to help them find new positions. As a result, many years later I'm still in contact with many of those employees whom I had to let go.

Many people take the opposite approach when they let someone go. Instead of trying to make it as easy as possible on the person about to be fired, they try to get it over with as quickly as possible in order to make it as easy as possible on themselves. Jose was just the opposite. He kept the focus on the other person. Amazingly, even though he was in a position where he had to let people go practically weekly, word of how he treated people got around, and no one ever seemed to fear him or dislike him. Stuff happens—markets change, jobs get eliminated, people don't always live up to expectations. People understand that, but I think they also prefer to work for and with people they respect. The way Jose handled the worst of situations made it easy to respect him. It comes back to something as simple as the Golden Rule. Treat people the way you would like to be treated; fire them the way you would like to be fired—with as much grace and respect as you can manage, and with a focus on humanity not humiliation.

When Bad Results Are Misleading

One last word about recognizing bad results: Make sure you don't punish people for something that isn't really their fault. Sometimes there is an unforeseeable change in the market. Sometimes leadership has set objectives that need to be adjusted. Penalizing people for not making their numbers when there was little if anything they could have done is not going to help you build a meritocracy.

One year, one of divisions at the company I was working for

didn't perform well. As a result, no one within the entire division was eligible for a year-end bonus. However, leadership recognized that there were a handful of individuals who had done a very good job throughout the year, and without their contributions the numbers could have been a lot worse. As a result, the decision was made to privately and quietly give those individuals discretionary bonuses to say thank you for their hard work even though the brand as a whole didn't hit its objectives. This is an important thing to think about because you don't want to suddenly discourage people or lose your best people just because times are tough or results are down—maybe *especially* in these situations. After all, that is when you need your best people the most.

Leaders need to strike a balance in this way. You obviously can't be rewarding poor or mediocre performance on a regular basis. It makes the bonus a useless tool if it can be expected regardless of results. But you also have to look at the full picture and make sure you are always being fair in a meritocracy.

Be Clear About Your Whys

This idea goes back to watching your shadow. Whenever you are considering recognizing someone or letting someone go, stop for a minute and ask yourself what message you are sending with your actions and choices. Then ask yourself if that message is clear to everyone affected by your decision. If the reasons behind your decisions aren't clear, then they can feel arbitrary or personal to people—like you are rewarding someone who doesn't really deserve it or disciplining someone just because you don't like that person. Most of us have worked in offices where stories like these have made the rounds. Sometimes it's a matter of jealousy or outsized expectations on someone's part when they do, but often it's simply a matter of not making the reasons clear. Remember, as a leader you are always onstage and your actions always send a message — whether you mean for them to or not.

Score Yourself on Leading Edge #3: Dream Big, Work Hard

For each of the questions that follow, answer Yes, No, or Sometimes. At the end of each section, add up the number of answers that fall in each of these three categories.

Dream Big

1. Do you consider motivating and inspiring people to be one of the most important aspects of your job?

2. Do you actively avoid leading by intimidation?

3. Do you regularly help your team members pursue personal goals?

4. Do you regularly look for ways that the company can support your team members' personal goals?

5. Do your people feel that you care about them?

6. Do you actively look for clues that people might be struggling and look for ways to help?

7. Do you help your people strike a healthy work-life balance?

8. Do you create fun, shared experiences in your workplace?

9. Do you help your people feel that they are part of something bigger than themselves and contributing to a greater whole?

10. Would others describe you as authentic in your attempts to motivate and inspire?

Work Hard

1. Do you formally recognize people for their accomplishments on a regular basis?

2. Do you regularly look for opportunities to spontaneously recognize people when you catch them doing something right?

3. Do you have a recognition award that is attention-grabbing, memorable, and fun?

4. Are salaries and bonuses obviously tied to merit and not to things like politics or length of service?

5. When you reward people, do you make sure they are living up to the company's values as well as achieving admirable results?

6. Do you work to create a culture of meritocracy by promoting transparency and objectivity?

7. Do you work to create a culture of meritocracy by being fair and balanced in the way you treat and measure people?

8. Do you address bad results honestly and directly, without dwelling on them when they have been remedied?

9. Do you manage out poor performers and do it in a way that can be respected by everyone — the people being let go and those who remain with the company?

10. When you recognize someone, do you make crystal clear to that person and to everyone else *why* you are doing it?

Score Yourself

Look back at each No or Sometimes answer that you gave. These are your areas of opportunity. Pick a few areas to work on, and over the next quarter think about ways that you can turn those Nos into Sometimes and those Sometimes into Yeses. Do this quarter after quarter, and it will be like you are doing performance reviews on your own leadership skills and abilities. Pay attention to how you change from quarter to quarter and how dreaming big and working hard affects business results.

Your Top Five

Below, list five things you can work on over the next quarter to improve your score for Leading Edge #3: Dream Big, Work Hard.

1.

2.

3.

4.

5.

LEADING EDGE #4:
TRUST BUT VERIFY

7: Trust—Believe in People

Henry Ford once said something that goes right to the heart of how crucial belief is to achieving success in any context: "Whether you think you can or whether you think you can't, you're right." This quote refers to people's belief in themselves, but from the leader's perspective, the same could be said of your view of the people you lead: Whether you think *they* can or whether you think *they* can't, you are probably right.

No leader will make it very far without a belief in people. Why? Because no man is an island, as they say, and no leader will make it very far without the help and contributions of others. In fact, a leader without followers can't really be called a leader at all. And anytime you set out to do something on a large scale—whether it's in a corporation, the military, a university, or any setting where a there is a group of people—the question will always arise of how you get people to work together in a committed way toward the same ends.

The answer to that eternal question begins with leaders investing their trust and belief in the people they need to succeed. These are essential components of doing great things together and getting leading-edge results. Just to be clear, I'm not talking about blind trust here—trust needs to be built with open and discerning eyes (that is what the *verify* part of *trust but verify* is all about, and I will talk about it in the next chapter). Before leaders can verify results, they must know how to create conditions under which people can and want to succeed, conditions that breed the following characteristics:

- A shared sense of loyalty

- More investment and engagement by team members

- More honest and open communication

- A more positive and supportive work environment

- Less pressure on the leader to make things happen alone

If you think about it, it's really common sense. Anything you accomplish together as a team or organization starts with a belief that the thing can be done. Leaders can do a lot to inspire a can-do attitude in their people by believing in their abilities and intentions and trusting them to deliver. Conversely, they can do a lot to undermine that spirit f they aren't careful. Believing in people and building a trusting relationship with them takes effort, but leaders with an edge understand that it's well worth the effort.

Why It's So Important to Trust and Believe in People

Over the course of his career as an entrepreneur, my dad has been able to witness many of the benefits of trust and belief that I listed above. He started his business with a handful of employees in the early 1970s and grew it to a place where he had four hundred employees across seven companies generating $100 million in sales.

Today, because the political and economic problems in Venezuela have taken their toll, he is back to having only fifteen employees. The remarkable thing is that the fifteen people who remain are the same fifteen employees that he started with. They have stuck around for upward of forty years, throughout a whole lot of changes that have included both ups and downs. These people have invested practically their entire lives in him and his business, and my father always keeps that thought top of mind. He feels a tremendous sense of loyalty to these people, and they have shown him the same in return—in fact, it's the most remarkable example of a shared sense of loyalty that I have ever heard of. You don't get that kind of committed, longstanding relationship without trust and belief in one another.

On a one-on-one level, when you have employees or colleagues whom you trust and who trust you, it makes you feel more invested in one another and in your shared success. It also promotes open and honest communication. People are better able to accept feedback, even critical feedback, and are more likely to be honest with you in return when you are getting off track or about to make a mistake. It makes it more pleasant to be around one another, and you will feel more willing to help one another out. It doesn't matter what the context is, when you have the support of trusted people it makes your job that much easier to do.

Beyond all that, there is a personal benefit to the leader: It's simply a more fulfilling way to live and to lead. When you don't believe in people, you cut yourself off from them in important ways. That can make you feel isolated and alone. It tends to increase your stress level when you don't have people around you can count on. I think most of us know that being cynical, wary, and distrustful of others is not the best way to lead a happy, well-adjusted life. What I think too many people don't realize is that it's not the best way to be successful in life either.

What a Lack of Trust Can Do

In my experience when an organization or team lacks a basic belief in people, the effect is pretty obvious. I always think of Patrick Lencioni's bestseller *The Five Dysfunctions of a Team*. In that book, the absence of trust is dysfunction number one, the first key problem that gets in the way and steers teams off track.

I also think back to instances when I saw the effect personally. I have worked in companies where I watched dysfunctional teams get caught up in squabbles and backstabbing rather than healthy disagreements and competition. It's obvious how much it upsets people, saps their energy, and pulls their focus from more important business objectives. Rather than looking at where the business is headed and watching the bottom line, they get caught up in power dynamics and petty rivalries. Instead of improving because of the support and contributions of others, leaders can easily be undermined in an environment like this. It doesn't bring out the best in leaders or in the people they lead.

When I first started working at Burger King, it was right after the company had been acquired by 3G Capital. The organization was going through a restructuring as a result of the acquisition, which left a lot of people feeling uneasy and distrustful of the leadership as they wondered whether it would mean transfers, demotions, or even the loss of their jobs. I was brought in during this time as an outsider to help with the restructuring, which meant that practically all of my team members were wary of me from the start. Many questioned my intentions and whether I knew enough about the company or about them to make the right decisions. One man even came up to me in my first week to tell me that he believed he should have gotten my job. Of course, any time a new leader comes onboard that person has some trust building to do, but this was beyond the norm.

What I came to discover was that this distrustful atmosphere had been around for a long time, even before the acquisition. Remember, this was a business in decline, which was why I was challenged to turn the business around in six months or get fired. It was clear to me that this lack of trust was a big part of what had been holding it back. What's more, we were never going to be able to make the big changes we needed to make in the short time we had to make them if we were too busy fighting each other.

The first thing I did was make it clear to everyone that I didn't have a secret agenda. My only objective was to do what I had been brought in to do, which was to turn the business around. I also made it clear that everyone needed to have that as their main objective if they wanted to stay. You were either on my team or you weren't, and I was going to give everyone an equal chance to show me where they stood.

I also had a very direct conversation with the man who said he should have my job. I told him I understood where he was coming from—no one likes to lose out on a promotion—but the situation was what it was. "I know you wanted this position, but they didn't pick you," I told him. "They picked me, and we either make the best out of this or we part ways."

What I have discovered over the years is that while trust will never happen all at once, you can always start to build it by being open and honest with people—even, or especially, when you have uncomfortable things to say to them. You begin with that honesty and then you set clear objectives and expectations, so there are no gray areas. If you follow up in a fair and consistent way, then you will have done what you can to lay a foundation. You can then step back and give people space to decide what they want to do. They will either live up to your expectations or they won't. (More on how to handle it if they don't in the coming sections.)

At Burger King, my team members more than lived up to expectations—even the person who wanted my job. Within ninety days, the business was already on an upswing, so was the trust level among the team. I think it comes down to the Golden Rule once again. Treat people the way you want to be treated. By the same token, lead people the way you want to be led. All people want someone to believe in them. All people want someone they can trust. As a leader, your trust and belief are two of the most powerful tools you have to offer.

5 Essentials for Building Trust

- Be open and honest with people—transparency is key

- Be clear about your expectations—no gray areas

- Do what you say you are going to do—follow through

- Have one set of standards for everyone, including yourself—remember your shadow

- All of the above, over and over again—consistency, consistency, consistency

Give Trust to Get Trust, or Trust Is a Two-Way Street

In the most productive relationships, trust is a two-way street. This doesn't mean you can't be cutthroat at times. You may still fire people, put pressure on people, set high expectations. Doing these things and trusting people are not mutually exclusive. However, you position yourself to get back more from people if you are also willing to give.

Some leaders don't agree with this. Some believe that they must use intimidation or fear to try to push people. I have talked about leading by intimidation before, and one of the things that is so counterproductive about this approach is what it does to trust. I once knew an executive who would openly say, "I want people to be afraid of me. I want people walking around here worried that they might get fired at any moment." Would you trust someone who says things like that?

This kind of approach pits a leader against his people instead of everyone feeling that they are on the same side working toward the same end. It's a "me against them" approach instead of "we are in this together." If I'm not getting what I want from a team member, my first step is not to threaten or instill fear. That's just misplaced energy in my view, a sure way to encourage people to brush up their résumés so they can look for a new job instead of focusing on the problem at hand. Instead, I will sit down with the person, analyze together what is going on, and create a plan for making changes that can be quantified and measured. Then we will keep at it—keep monitoring the issue, keep making adjustments, keep tracking the progress—until the issue is fixed. The difference here is between leaving people out in the cold and helping them understand they aren't alone. It's the difference between letting people sink and using your experience to help them swim. I choose to help people swim— for their own sake, for the team's sake, for the organization's sake, even for my sake—because the failure of one person affects all the rest. Of course, the approach I take is more work. It's easy to simply tell people what they need to do. It's harder to help them figure out how to get there. It's harder, but a lot more effective.

I once saw the great Colin Powell, whose leadership experience ranges from the military to the highest levels of the federal government, talk about the key characteristic of effective leadership. "It ultimately comes down to creating conditions of trust within an organization," he said. "Good leaders are people who are trusted by followers."

In terms of how to establish trust, Powell made clear that it has to start with the leader. If you want to be able to trust people, you have to make sure that they can trust you. He said:

You prepare the followers. You train them. You give them what they need to get the job done. Don't give them a job if you're not going to give them the resources. And you're prepared to take the risks with them.

So they would teach us at the infantry school: no matter how cold it is, lieutenant, you must never look cold. No matter how hungry you all are, lieutenant, you must never appear hungry. No matter how terrified you are, lieutenant, you must never look terrified. Because if you are scared, tired, hungry, and cold... they will be scared, tired, hungry and cold...

They'll follow you into the darkest night, down the deepest valley, and up the highest hill if they trust you. So, the essence of leadership is about doing all that the science of management says you can with resources, but taking that extra step and giving it that spark. That spark comes from getting people to trust you...

That is epitome of the "we're in this together" approach. Trust is built in the trenches, when you get in there with people, show them (what you want them to do, how you want them to act—instead of just telling them "do this or you're fired." Trust is built when your leader is right there with you no matter what is happening. When people trust you, they almost always become trustworthy in return. That is when they start putting pressure on themselves to be competitive, live up to expectations, achieve greatness instead of you having to do it for them. You won't have to say, "You need to do this, or else," because they already understand what needs to be done, and they are right there with you in doing it.

Taking a Risk

Risk-taking is a big part of business. You invest in product development in the hopes that you will come up with the next money-making innovation. You might buy a failing company with the belief that you can turn it around. Most leaders make risk versus reward calculations all the time. What many don't think about, however, is the fact that placing your trust in people is its own kind of (necessary) risk.

When I started my own business, I remember feeling this keenly because I was the one in the position of needing people to take a risk on me. I started my agency from nothing, so on day one it was just me. I didn't have any employees. I didn't have any clients. The first thing I needed was to get people to trust that my new company was worth investing their time in, if they were going to become employees, or their money in, if they were going to become clients. That basically meant getting people to put their trust in me. At that stage I *was* the company.

In many ways, trusting someone for the first time is like taking leap of faith. I will never forget the first person to take a chance on me and my new company. It was a guy at Sony Electronics. He graduated from Northwestern, as I did, so when I pitched him my services, he gave me a chance. He started me on a very small project as a test, and I did a good job. Then I got another project that was a little bit bigger. Soon he had put my company on retainer. That gave me enough of a foundation to expand and hire more people. He took a chance, basically trusting me because we had gone to the same school and knew some people in common. I was so appreciative that I worked extra hard to make sure he wasn't sorry that he had put his faith in me.

It was the same with my employees. Trying to get employees to join a startup can be hard. They want to know what's in it for them. They worry about the stability of the company, about whether you are going to be able to pay their salaries. Even though I have moved on, I still talk to many of my former employees because we built strong relationships based on mutual trust.

Trusting and believing in people can be risky. I could have let that Sony executive down. I could have let my new employees down. I didn't, but they didn't know for sure that I wouldn't when they first placed their trust in me. Because it feels risky, some leaders avoid it. They prefer to micromanage their people so they can feel that they are in control. I think leaders who do this are really risk-averse. They are afraid to take a chance on something that isn't a sure thing. And let's face it, people are never sure things.

But think of it this way: You never would have gotten where you are today if you didn't have some belief in yourself, which is an act of faith too. That was certainly true for me. After Chavez came into power in Venezuela in the late 1990s, the country's fortunes took a downturn, as did my father's business. It was my father's idea that I come to the United States to study, but it was my idea to stay. I wanted to see if I could make it in the largest economy in the world.

Of course, as all immigrants know, venturing to another country is a risk, an act of faith; you have to trust your own abilities, believe that you can find your way, and succeed in an unknown place. For me, I found that faith through my belief in God and trusting His plan over my life (Jer. 29:11): "For I know the plans I have for you," declares the Lord, "plans to prosper you and not to harm you, plans to give you hope and a future." The example of my immigrant parents, who came from Europe to Venezuela to forge new lives for themselves without any money, family, friends, practically anything, helped me too. My faith and my background gave me the belief in myself that I needed to succeed. That, in turn, showed me the importance of trusting and believing in other people.

That's what worked for me personally, but regardless of your experience, it's crucial for all leaders to find a way to cultivate their belief. Believing in people and believing in yourself are both leaps of faith. You put the hope out there first and then try to meet it. But if you don't start there, you won't be able to move beyond your current limitations to try out new ideas, build new relationships, explore new territories — the kinds of things that can really give you that edge to succeed.

Belief is only a starting place, and there is more work to do, but if you don't have the belief, you are definitely not going to get there. It's like it was with my new company — if that one executive from Sony hadn't trusted me enough to get me started, I never would have had a company at all.

Belief As an Investment in People

Believing in people often means investing in them before you are sure of the return you are going to get. This kind of risk-taking is a key trait of any truly successful leader. Belief is motivating. Belief is inspiring. It's also the best chance you have of getting real results.

By the way, it also feels good to invest in people, to help them out, to make a difference in their lives. If you are able to use your position and abilities to give back to people and really make an impact, it's motivating not just for them but for you. Being a leader is not always easy. It can be a lot of pressure day after day. It can be lonely being the one in charge. It's important to think about how to keep your people going and how to keep yourself going too.

The Reverend Chip Edens, of Christ Church in Charlotte, uses a model for investing in people—what he would call "using your gifts to help others"—that I have found very useful throughout my career and my life. He calls it the 3Ts, which stand for

1.   Time

2.   Treasure

3.   Talent, or expertise

I have personally made use of each one of these, and seen others effectively do the same. In the following sections, we will look at each of these opportunities to invest in people, one by one, and how you can make use of them yourself.

Time

One of the most cost-effective ways of showing people you believe in them is by investing your time in them. That can mean something as simple as finding the time to grab lunch or coffee with junior people in your organization, or a bigger time commitment like an ongoing mentorship. When I have left companies in the past, I have had a lot of younger people reach out to me to say that that was what they were going to miss the most—that one-on-one time I spent with them, just getting to know who they were and what their dreams and goals were, occasionally offering some coaching or advice. You might be surprised how much a little focused time and attention means to people.

Not long ago, I met a young man who had recently earned his MBA. He was a smart guy, obviously, but he had immigrated to this country as I had many years before and was trying to figure out how best to handle the job application process. Because of his education, he was getting multiple offers. However, the company he wanted to work for the most had made him an offer for a position that had a lot less responsibility and paid a lot less money than the one he had applied for. He didn't know what to do, so he asked me for some advice.

I had only met this young man twice in my life, but he seemed like a good person. Besides, I remembered what it was like to come from another country, just starting out, and trying to make it here. I had gotten plenty of help from people along the way, so I wanted to help him, to pay it forward.

I called him up and coached him on how to respond to the offer he wanted to accept: I explained why I didn't think it was fair, gave him suggestions—what he could say to get more responsibility and compensation—and advised him on what to do if the company didn't budge. It took all of half an hour, and he was able to negotiate a better offer and start his career on a much better note.

You can use your time to invest in people outside the office as well. I sit on a planning committee at our church, which is a volunteer position but allows me to share thoughts on the impact the church will have in the community over the next twenty to twenty-five years. Hopefully the efforts of the committee will help our church continue to grow and become more relevant to a wider group of people.

Treasure

By treasure, I basically mean money. In business you invest treasure in people in terms of their salaries. You can give them bonuses when they excel. These are obvious but still important ways of showing people you believe in them, which are not to be underestimated. After all, many people use their compensation packages as a way of keeping score and evaluating how much the company values them.

Besides these obvious ways, there are other ways to use treasure to invest in people. You can invest in employees with extra time off. You can invest in a community by creating new jobs or opening a new office or plant. A company can also invest treasure in charitable causes that matter to their employees, customers, and other constituents. When I was at Yum! Brands, the company invested a lot of resources in the UN's World Food Program. Driven Brands chose to support the Children's Miracle Network, which was a favorite among employees.

You may be surprised how much these kinds of investments mean to people—and not just those receiving the funds. Research shows that millennial workers in particular tend to look closely at how companies are giving back to their local communities, and to the world as a whole, before deciding whether to work for them. They increasingly want the philanthropy of the organization they work for to reflect their own values. It's a subject that comes up often in my interviews with young people.

Recently, I had drinks with one of my mentors. He recently donated a couple million dollars to his alma mater, the University of North Carolina, and in return the university named a program in its business school in his honor. He is in his mid-fifties now, and the donation was about giving back what he believed his degree had helped him gain throughout his career. He will never have that money again, but from an investment standpoint, he gets the satisfaction of seeing the school grow and knowing it can continue to affect the lives of young people as it did for him.

I once heard the then CEO of Colgate give a speech at Harvard in which he said something that really stuck with me. He said (and I'm paraphrasing here) that you spend your entire professional life collecting power and wealth, and as soon as you reach the top, you start giving it away. That was why he was donating his money to different endowments and spending his time lecturing at universities. The guy probably spent thirty years climbing the corporate ladder to get to the point where he was head of an iconic worldwide organization. And once he got to a point where there wasn't much more to gain, he decided it was time to start giving. It was such a powerful thought. On some level, all of us think about our legacies to some degree, which is not the same as thinking about the return we will get on the treasure we invest. It's a natural human instinct to want to give back. It's also a natural human instinct to trust and respect those who do so.

Talent

By talent, I mean your knowledge or expertise. If you are at a point in your career where you have risen to become a leader, or are poised to do so, then you must have some experience to share.

I talked earlier about creating a personal board of directors to help steer your career and the benefit to be gained from the direction and honest feedback of your board members. If you are considering this advice, think about how much you will have gained from the expertise of others in this context or from people who have mentored you. It might be time to do the same for someone else. When I coached that young graduate who was entertaining his first job offers, it was an investment of time and talent.

I recently joined the board of directors of a nonprofit in my area called Discovery Place, which is a children's science museum. They have four locations in North Carolina and wanted to make use of my expertise in working with franchise businesses to help them better structure their back office and leverage their resources across locations. This book is another example of making use of one's talent. It was my desire to use what I had learned to help grow and develop young leaders that motivated me to create a leadership program, which then turned into *Leading with Edge*.

Ways to Invest Your 3Ts

- Mentor or be on someone's personal board of directors

- Be a sounding board or listening ear

- Coach someone less experienced than you through a difficult decision

- Make a donation to a charitable cause

- Donate your time and expertise to a good cause

When Your Investment Doesn't Pay Off

Because it's a kind of risk-taking, your investment in people is never going to be a sure thing. That's okay. Investing in the stock market isn't a sure thing either, but it's still a wise thing to do with your money if you do it in a sensible way. If you choose wisely and take calculated risks, then more often than not, you will get a return on your investment whether you are talking about people or capital.

When I got to Burger King and that team member told me he thought he should have my job, we talked it out and went on to have a productive relationship. However, that wasn't the only time that happened to me. At another organization, a similar thing occurred when someone under me hierarchically openly wanted my position. I didn't have a problem with that at first. There is nothing wrong with some healthy ambition. However, as time went on, I discovered that wasn't his only issue. He was openly confrontational with people at meetings, causing a lot of tension and bad feelings. He was also deceptive at times, keeping information to himself that others could have benefited from. He just wasn't a team player, and in my view his results weren't good enough to merit more chances, so I talked to my boss about transferring him from my department or even letting him go.

Before it got to that point, however, I did my best to form an open, trusting, and productive working relationship. Over time, his negative intentions only intensified and began to poison morale among my team. By that point, my belief in him was gone and there was nothing left to invest in this relationship. It was time for him to go.

The experience taught me some lessons, first of which was to watch my back a bit more closely. You do have to keep your eyes open and verify that people are doing the right things. Sometimes people who seemed to be your greatest advocates will show you that they were really driving towards their own agenda. That doesn't mean you can't work with those people, but you will probably never gain back the same level of trust.

Live and learn, right? I could have come out of that situation with a real cynicism about people, believing that to get ahead and stay ahead, you can't trust anyone, but I still see the value of believing in people. When I'm feeling cynical, I remind myself of all the benefits you get from believing in people and creating relationships based on trust. Those benefits don't go away just because of one bad experience. Or even two bad experiences. I also believe that everyone deserves the benefit of the doubt until they do something to prove you wrong.

Maintaining Your Belief

Because trust and belief are so important, leaders need to take it upon themselves to cultivate these principles. They need to take responsibility for doing this even though things happen to all of us, which at times leave us feeling cynical and distrustful.

When I was invited to appear on an episode of the CBS show *Undercover Boss*, I went undercover in Maaco stores within the Driven Brands system to find out more about what it was really like to work for our company. I wasn't really a car guy when I started with Driven Brands, so there was a lot about the front-line business that I didn't know. I posed as a potential new hire for a range of jobs, including auto body technician (working to get out those dents and dings), car painter, detailer, and lot manager, a position that required spending my days organizing the lot and keeping track of the cars. I spent the day with people who had done these jobs for years, trying to keep up with them, and the experience was eye-opening.

Of all the people I worked with that day, only one made it pretty clear that he shouldn't be trusted. He revealed a habit of cutting corners and not upholding company standards in order to increase his margins. The others, who came from varied backgrounds, worked hard and did exceptional jobs, sometimes under truly difficult circumstances. The lot manager, for example, had to work outside in all kinds of weather, running across the lot to quickly retrieve cars for waiting customers despite a chronic bad back. The experience led me to think about ways I could show my belief in these team members by doing something truly meaningful for them.

If you have seen the show, then you know it ends by revealing to all the employees that their new trainee was actually the boss. The "undercover boss" then rewards or reprimands the employees based on his experiences with them. The guy who cut corners got a thirty-day warning to change his ways. The others, however, had shown me how difficult their jobs—and their lives—could be, so I wanted to do something to make things easier and reward their work. For the lot manager with the bad back, I had a covered workstation built so he wouldn't have to be outside in the heat or cold all the time. I also gave him a sizable bonus. For the detailer who had talked about how he worked hard for his family, I established a college fund for his kids and sent him on a family vacation. For the painter who took so much pride in his work, I made sure he was debt-free for the birth of his daughter and offered to personally coach him in business so that he might be able to open his own franchise one day.

The company and I invested all three Ts in these team members— time, talent, and especially treasure. The results of our investments, however, were a little bit puzzling over time. After a couple of years, all but one of those employees had left the company. We had given so much to them, so it came as a disappointment to see them walk away.

Sometimes maintaining your belief in people takes work. It's times like these when I personally pause and take stock. I would have loved it if all the people I worked with that day had become star employees for years to come, but that wasn't what happened. Still, it's important not to diminish the return we did get on our investment that day.

And what did I get in return? There was the satisfaction of making a difference in people's lives, which cannot be underestimated. There was the pride our entire organization took in seeing our company highlighted on TV. I also got a lot of insight into how things worked in our stores and what the challenges were. Those employees gave me a crash course in the good, the bad, and the ugly in our stores, from how someone could cut corners to make more in commissions to the struggles some of our employees go through to make ends meet and put food on the table for their families. It was humbling to see how difficult their jobs were—and how bad I was at them. It taught me to be more caring and to see things from a different perspective, which I hope made me a better leader overall.

Beyond that, Christian, the painter I started coaching and the only one who still worked for Driven Brands when I left the company, came up with a great idea — to start a bilingual training program in order to pull in a larger pool of potential talent among our franchise owners. We took the idea and ran with it, translating all our training materials and teaching the onboarding class for franchisees in Spanish when we had enough interest. These were big changes we made while I was there, and the program was a real success. In just a couple years, it grew to the point where we were onboarding more than 10 percent of our system using the new bilingual training. We may not have gotten exactly what we wanted out of the experience, but we got plenty. I remind myself of that whenever my belief in people starts to wane.

If you have had an experience that is making you distrustful of people, or if you are naturally cynical, I think you can still learn to believe. Putting your faith in somebody is a risk, but people can learn to take more risks little by little. After all, leadership itself is something that is learned over the years. As a leader, it's essential that you keep a realistic perspective. A bad experience doesn't negate all the good ones. A bad apple doesn't mean the whole orchard should be burned to the ground. This goes back to the start of this book and the concept of self-knowledge. The more you monitor your reactions to things and the more you are aware of the shadow you are casting, the more you can do to cultivate a more productive attitude. If you are really struggling, look for opportunities to actively cultivate your belief in people by doing charity work. Spend some time with people who are good at cultivating trusting relationships and learn from them. Leaders with edge are aware of what might be getting in their way — and they do something about it.

More people are well-intentioned than not; you don't want to cut off those who are worth trusting. We all get burned by people from time to time. I certainly have been. But that doesn't mean that in my next role I changed my leadership principles. I was a bit more cautious about who I trusted going forward: I didn't change who I was or my basic values.

There is a risk in believing in people, but it's a risk leaders need to be willing to take if they truly want to make an impact. If you really want to move things forward, you can't do it by yourself. You need other people, so you have to take a risk on people doing the right thing, willing to work for the success of the whole, not just for them-selves.

8: Verify—Build Trust Through Accountability

Trust is essential for successful leadership, but it's also something that isn't, or shouldn't be, given blindly or all at once. Trust is something you build and something you can promote through accountability.

"Trust but verify" is a phrase that Ronald Reagan used during the Cold War when speaking about his relations with Soviet President Mikhail Gorbachev and the USSR. This is the same lens through which I look at trust among my team members. Trust doesn't mean being hands-off and letting people do what they do. More often it means monitoring their progress so they are held accountable for what you are trusting them to achieve. In fact, when Reagan used the phrase after he and Gorbachev had signed the Intermediate-Range Nuclear Forces Treaty (INF Treaty), in which the two countries agreed to eliminate many of their nuclear and conventional missiles, he was describing the extensive, multiyear verification process the two sides had come up with to monitor compliance with the treaty's terms.

The two countries knew they had to check up on one another. At the same time, the relationship between Reagan and Gorbachev led to big changes. And that's important too. If you start out by assuming that people aren't capable of something, then you cut off the possibility that they are. A balance needs to be struck, and that is what this chapter is all about.

Use What You Already Know

We have covered a lot of territory so far. If you have been following the advice in this book, then you already have a lot of tools you can use to verify trust and drive accountability among your team members or across your organization. In the first section, I talked about the importance of gaining knowledge about the people you lead. If you have done that, then you have begun to build relationships that will help establish trust. You will also have a better understanding of the goals, strengths, and weaknesses of each person who reports to you; you know what to look out for.

In the second section, I talked about setting goals and expectations. If those have been made clear and everyone understands them, then it's going to be that much easier to verify whether people are on track and deserving your trust. There will be mutual agreement about the results people are expected to deliver. Everyone will be familiar with the measuring stick and how you will be monitoring their progress, so there will be few surprises.

In the previous section, I talked about motivating and rewarding people in a consistent, transparent way. If you have treated people equally and rewarded based on merit—not because of friendship, length of service, or any other subjective measure—then your team members will trust you to recognize good work and reward it fairly. In this way, you will have begun to build a culture of trust among all your people. As I mentioned in the last chapter, trust helps foster open, honest communication, which makes the verification process that much easier. You won't have to catch someone doing something wrong very often because most everything will already be out in the open.

Each of these pieces is part of a whole. They need to be used together in order to gain the edge you are looking for. If you have gotten this far in the book and are finding it difficult to verify results about your team members, look back at the assessments at the end of each section and see if there is something you are missing.

Incremental Trust

Too often people think about trust in absolute terms: You either trust someone or you don't. But the smart leader knows that trust is something that is built over time, piece by piece. It's also something that is constantly monitored because the person you trust today may fall tomorrow. This isn't meant to be some sort of sinister outlook in which you are always looking over your shoulder assuming someone is ready to stab you in the back at any moment. It's simply meant to take into account that the people you lead are human. They are experienced in some areas and lack experience in others. They have strengths and they have weaknesses. They have good days and they have bad ones. Leaders with edge don't punish people for simply being human. They put process and discipline in place so that mistakes or missteps don't have cataclysmic consequences.

Instead of thinking about trust as some sort of leap into the unknown, think of it as a process of inching forward. This philosophy works for new employees, for people who are growing into more responsibility, and even for those people you have known for a while (as a way to continue to ensure that your trust is well placed).

I remember a clear example of being on the receiving end of incremental trust early in my career, when I was brand manager at KFC. I was young and eager to take on more responsibility. I also had a passion for the customer experience, so I went to the head of my division, Scott Bergen, then chief marketing officer, and asked if I could work to improve the customer experience at KFC. He said I could, as long as I did it as a side project and still kept up my day-to-day duties. Those were the clear conditions he set. Then he monitored my progress along the way. I started out by gathering data on organizations that had successfully changed their customer experience in ways that significantly affected the bottom line. I looked at places as diverse as the Ritz Carlton and Chick-fil-A, analyzed my findings, and presented them to Bergen. He was impressed by the work I had done and thought I was onto something, so he made customer experience my full-time position.

This approach relies on open and honest communication. At KFC, I trusted Bergen enough to go to him with my aspirations. In return, rather than shutting me down and telling me to stick to what I knew, he trusted me enough to give me a shot, even though what I wanted to do was outside my job description. Then he was clear about what I needed to do to continue to merit his trust and earn more of it. He gave me the freedom to get the work done in whatever way I saw fit, but he monitored my progress and his door was always open to me so I could ask for help or advice.

It was Bergen who had established this dynamic that made the "trust but verify" process work so well, and he did that from the very beginning. I first met him when he came to Northwestern, where I was in graduate school, to recruit new talent. He was very personable, engaging, high energy, and easy to talk to. He made it clear that he wanted to build a relationship with those of us whom he was considering recruiting. He actively took an interest in people and made it clear that they could come to him with ideas, questions, even complaints. When a group of us started our new jobs, he said to us,

"All of you are going to go on to do great things in this company." I believed him and was motivated by him.

That was why, when I saw a need to improve KFC's customer service and had an idea for how to work on it, I went to Bergen to talk about it. I was a senior analyst at the time, which meant that Bergen, who was CMO, was my boss's boss's boss's boss's boss's boss. There were about six layers of hierarchy between us. I obviously asked permission from my supervisor before going to him, but he was the kind of person who valued open and honest communication as well, so he told me to go ahead. That open-door policy that Bergen and other leaders at KFC upheld made trusting and verifying trust a lot easier for everyone.

Incremental Trust Builds Confidence and Ability

Building trust slowly and steadily over time, and verifying results along the way, is something a leader needs to do drive accountability. And it has an added benefit: It's a great process to use to build skills and confidence among your team members.

I experienced this myself recently when I volunteered through my church to build a home for Habitat for Humanity. When I showed up at the construction site, I had no idea what I would be doing. I like to build things, but I don't consider myself a particularly handy man, and I had no previous experience in construction whatsoever. So I was wondering how helpful I would actually be.

Still, I decided to give it my best effort. I was part of a group of around fifty people, and I immediately gravitated to this older gentleman — maybe because with his long white hair and beard he looked like an extremely fit version of Santa Claus. His name was Powell and he was a builder by trade. I didn't want to mess anything up, so I told him about my lack of experience. Then I said to him, "But other than that, I can help you with whatever you need."

Powell gave me a belt, a handful of nails, and a hammer and then said, "Just follow me." The basic structure and the outside walls of the house had already been erected, but that was about it. I followed Powell around the house, hammering nails wherever he told me to. Pretty soon I could see the results of our work. We had put up beams and started on the divisions between rooms.

Powell was very patient and stuck with me the entire day, giving me a small task, making sure I did it exactly as he told me to, and then giving me another. After a time, I felt like I was getting the hang of it. He must have too because he stopped watching me so closely. Then the tasks he gave me got a little bit harder. When that happened, he would watch closely again for a time until he was sure I was comfortable with them and doing them right.

It was a perfect example of "trust but verify." I learned so much that day in such a short period of time just by being accountable to someone with clear expertise and the willingness to share that expertise with me in a focused and consistent way — but not an overbearing way. The way he worked with me made me perform better. He took the time to teach me, answer my questions, and monitor my progress to make sure I wasn't messing anything up, but he let me do things, try things, and move on to harder things once I had gotten the hang of it. By the end of the day, he let me loose to work on a room by myself. By then, I was confident enough to be on my own. He came by when I was finished just to look everything over and make sure I had done okay. That was it.

In the wrong hands, you can easily see how the situation could have been a disaster, or just a waste of time. Instead, I was able to really contribute despite my lack of experience and relevant skills. It was quite a steep learning curve and resulted in such a positive experience, that I can't wait to help build another house someday soon.

Finding the Line Between Trusting and Verifying

As a leader, you always have to balance the needs of the whole—your team, your division, your organization, even yourself—all at once. This can get tricky at times. For example, letting something slide with one employee may seem empathetic at the time, but you have to weigh that against the effect it has on others. That decision to benefit one person may make the job more difficult for someone else or for the team. It may also serve to discourage people; after all, why work hard if failure doesn't have consequences? At the same time, not everyone is the same. Some people need more monitoring than others to stay on track, while others may be put off by too much oversight. How do you find that line?

It starts with knowing what approach best suits you as a leader. There is no one way to lead, and if you know your strengths and your style (this goes back to the self-knowledge I talked about in the first section), then you can put them to work here. Perhaps you are naturally more of a hands-on leader who likes to be copied or informed every step along the way as one of your direct reports works on something. Or maybe you prefer to give people more space, letting them find their own way and checking on their progress once a week or so. I have worked with and worked for both kinds of leaders and have seen both be successful. The key is to make clear to everyone what your approach is and then follow through on it.

Beyond that, you will need to make adjustments according to what works for the individuals you lead. It's important to remember that everyone is different. What motivates one person may not be what motivates someone else. Recognition may be a key driver for one person, while position and title may be for another. Yet another person may be driven almost entirely by money. This is where it really helps to know your people well. Spending time with people will give you a subjective read on them, but it's also a good idea to supplement that knowledge with the more objective perspective offered by formal assessment.

Making Use of Assessments

Doing formal assessments is a good way to get an understanding of someone's personality. There are a whole range of options out there when it comes to doing assessments — Myers-Briggs, Work Simply, Big Five, and many others. Some focus on behavior, others are more psychographic. Some are even free online so you don't have to spend a lot of money here, though I think it can be worth the investment to gain the more detailed insights that come from some of the for-pay products. They all paint a picture of what a person's strengths and weaknesses are and how that person likes to work, which is useful information for any leader to have.

At GrandVision, we have used Caliper, which tests how well a person matches his or her specific job function. You can customize the test so it's different for every position and every level, from entry level to leadership roles. It then gives you a percentage that indicates how well someone's personality fits the requirements of a given position.

You can also customize the test so it measures how well someone matches the values of your specific company. At GrandVision, we customize our test so it aligns its measurements with what we have determined to be five key areas: financial, growth, sales, operations, and people. The results of the test gauge how well that employee would perform in each area.

The results of this test give leaders a basic prediction of how well individuals would perform in their roles and how well they would fit within the culture of the organization. Then, when we do performance reviews, we can compare how well the person actually performed against the test's predictions. We also learned about different aspects of someone's personality. The test rates people on aspects like aggressiveness, assertiveness, ego drive, risk-taking, and urgency. These kinds of assessments are valuable tools to use when considering new hires. Beyond that, they give great insight into how to lead each of your team members. If someone rates a bit lower on the urgency scale, for example, you might want to keep a closer eye on him as he works on a project with a tight deadline.

Tactics for Verifying and Promoting Accountability

Being accountable isn't all that complicated, at least in theory. It's about the simple act of doing what you said you would do and communicating clearly that you did it. That's it. If that happens on a regular basis, then I know I can trust you. It's great when employees take it upon themselves to make sure this is happening, but it's the leader's job to make sure they do. Following are the basic steps for driving accountability with any team member.

1) *Get to know the person*: This is your starting place, which will give you the information you need to move forward. You can do this through a combination of spending one-on-one time with the person in order to form a subjective opinion and having the person take an assessment test, so you have some objective, third-party data to work with. This gives you both qualitative (from your personal experience) and quantitative data from the assessment. Taken together, you will

have real insight into how best to work with this person and which areas may need to be monitored more closely.

2) *Set regular check-ins*: I personally like to be updated by each of my direct reports every couple of days, at least in the beginning of our relationship. After that, it may move to a weekly or biweekly check-in depending on performance. I make sure my direct reports are well aware of when those check-ins will happen and what is expected of them during our meetings. I expect people to come prepared. I want a thorough update on their projects, and I want them to be able to answer questions. Whenever possible, I also want to see the progress that has been made, not just hear about it.

3) *Compare data*: Compare the information you get from people during their regular check-ins against the data you are getting back about their results. That may be sales data, financial data, customer service surveys, internal surveys, or whatever applies to each specific job function. Make sure you verify the numbers and the less quantitative aspects: how well somebody fits into the culture, whether that person is a team player, or whether he/she is self-motivated. This requires you to gather information, either informally or through interviews, from other team members, the person's direct reports, vendors, customers, etc. All this happens in between quarterly performance reviews. In fact, when it comes time for a formal review, all the elements that go into your performance assessment should already be well known to you and to the person under review.

4) *Repeat, repeat, repeat*: Keep doing all these things over and over again. People change, so getting to know them is a process that never stops. Objectives evolve which is why check-ins are always necessary. And verifying what you think and what a person says against availa-

ble data is a best practice that will keep you on top of what is happening in your business and minimize surprises.

Trust Isn't Always a Straight Line

As you get to know people better and they demonstrate their ability to perform, you are likely to give them more and more leeway, more and more trust. Maybe you don't check in with them as often. Maybe you give them more responsibility, even a promotion. This is the way it should work, but you also have to be aware that people can sometimes do things that dial back the needle.

The story I told in chapter 6, about the woman who received a promotion and immediately started burning bridges in the department she was about to leave, is a good example. I had another team member who was always full of good news when we met for our check-ins, but pretty soon I noticed that he rarely offered proof of his accomplishments. He would say he had a productive meeting with a vendor, but then I never saw any results from that meeting. He would say he was close to closing a deal, and then the deal would fall apart. These things happen sometimes, but they shouldn't become a trend. When it happened too many times with this particular employee, I had to change the way we worked together.

The first thing to do is to make sure there is open communication. Make clear what the problem is and your expectation that it be fixed. Also listen to what the person has to say. Perhaps there is a valid explanation for the person's failing. It's important to find out what it is and whether your team member is aware of the problem and the reasons behind it.

Then go back to the tactical steps I outlined above. Make sure you really know this person, especially if the person has done something that surprised you. Start checking in more regularly: if you were on a weekly check-in schedule, do it semiweekly or every couple days for a while, as long as necessary for you to be certain that the issue you were having has been remedied. Check in with the data more often to make sure you are getting an accurate picture from this person.

After a time, if all has gone well and you are considering whether to restore more autonomy to someone, it's often a good idea to test that person a bit first. Assigning someone a special project is a great way to create a context for assessing them. It can expose a person to new challenges and new people, allowing you to watch how the person reacts. This is also a great tactic to use when you are considering a promotion for someone. I love to continuously test people because it gives me valuable insight into who they are and how they are performing right now. Motivations and behaviors can sometimes surprise you. They can also change with time.

When someone takes a step or two backward, it isn't the end of the world, and it doesn't mean that you can't eventually resume a trusting relationship. To err is human, as they say. But to allow an erring human to go unchecked is just bad business.

When Trust Is Broken

While building trust may not be a straight line, there are times when that line is simply broken and trust cannot be repaired. It's important to look out for these sorts of situations and handle them decisively because they say something important about your values as a leader and about the company's values as a whole. If someone makes a mistake and apologizes for it, then a second chance is usually merited. When someone lets you down, and then lies about it, it may be a situation where trust isn't worth trying to repair. The same may be true when someone lets you down time and time again.

There are different levels of trust, and there's a difference between trusting someone and placing your trust "in" someone. Several years ago, I hired a Vice President of Marketing who came with a reputation of being a rock star performer. A few months in, however, I noticed his results were not so rock star. We would sit down for a weekly check-in and align on an action plan, but then nothing would move. He seemed to have a hard time moving quickly and making decisions. I grew impatient with all of the follow-ups and lack of results. Ultimately, I realized I couldn't place my trust "in" him as a performer. Something similar happened at work when an employee was found to have sexually harassed a colleague. There is no second chance for behavior like that.

There are such things as deal-breakers in business and in our personal lives. These typically happen when someone doesn't just fall short or makes a mistake but breaks the code of ethics or violates core values. The person cheats, lies, harms someone, or puts someone in harm's way. It's important to have a zero tolerance policy in these instances because you can open yourself up to lawsuits if you don't deal with them quickly and because it sends a message to everyone in the organization. Trust is essential among any group of people, but it can also be fragile and shouldn't be taken lightly. Anyone who betrays that ideal should be held accountable.

It All Takes Time

In our fast-paced world, it's important to remember that some things can't be rushed too much. The foundations for productive human interactions take time to build. Trust will grow stronger the more days and months you work with someone. The more difficult experiences you get through together, the more you will be able to trust each other.

It's a continual process that never stops—putting your faith in people, verifying that it isn't misplaced, and then adjusting according to the results. This is the daily work of every leader. The difference between an okay leader and one with an edge often comes down to execution. Follow-through is what takes something from being simply a good idea and turns it into a habit that works consistently.

If fact, that advice applies to all of the lessons in this book. If you want to gain a serious edge in today's marketplace, one good feedback session with your people is not going to cut it. You can't just present them with challenges and then leave them at sea. You can't just take the time to build trust one month and then assume it will be there when you need it in the future. This strikes me as an area of leadership that isn't trumpeted enough. The day-to-day work of being a leader has more to do with the small actions you do on a regular basis — spending time with people, putting them on the right path, and making sure they are still on the right path a week, month, quarter, or year down the line — than any new idea or initiative you can come up with. This is what leading with an edge is all about. There is no substitute for it.

Score Yourself on Leading Edge #4:
Trust But Verify

For each of the questions that follow, answer Yes, No, or Sometimes. At the end of each section, add up the number of answers that fall in each of these three categories.

Trust

1. Do you trust the people on your team?

2. Do the people you work with trust you?

3. Do you regularly work to build trust among your team members and colleagues by being open and honest?

4. Do you regularly work to build trust among your team members and colleagues by being clear about your expectations?

5. Do you regularly work to build trust among your team members and colleagues by doing what you say you are going to do?

6. Do you regularly work to build trust among your team members and colleagues by having fair and evenly applied standards for everyone?

7. Do you understand that believing and trusting people are necessary risks you have to take?

8. Do you make a regular effort to invest your time in people?

9. Do you make a regular effort to invest your treasure in people?

10. Do you make a regular effort to invest your talent in people?

11. Do you look for ways to maintain a trusting attitude toward people even if you are sometimes disappointed in them?

12. Do make building trust and maintaining a belief in people priorities that you work on continuously?

Verify

1. Do you work to build trust in people over time?

2. Do you look for ways to increase confidence and ability as you build trust with people over time?

3. Do you strike a healthy balance between trusting people and looking over their shoulder to verify results?

4. Do you use assessments to gain insight into your people?

5. Do you spend regular time with each member of your team so that you can know them better?

6. Do you have regular check-ins set up with each of your direct reports?

7. Is each of your direct reports aware of what is required of them during those check-ins?

8. Do you regularly compare data against the information you are getting from people about their progress and performance?

9. Do you have a process in place to deal with occasions when someone doesn't perform up to expectations?

10. Do you know what constitutes a deal-breaker (those times when a second chance can't be given for a violation of trust) for you and your organization?

Score Yourself

Look back at each No or Sometimes answer that you gave. These are your areas of opportunity. Pick a few areas to work on, and over the next quarter think about ways that you can turn those Nos into Sometimes and those Sometimes into Yeses. Do this quarter after quarter, and it will be like you are doing performance reviews on your own leadership skills and abilities. Pay attention to how you change from quarter to quarter and how "trust but verify" skills affect business results.

Your Top Five

Below, list five things you can work on over the next quarter to improve your score for Leading Edge #4: Trust But Verify.

1.

2.

3.

4.

5.

Afterword:
The Best Advice I Could Ever Give

Early in my career, I had this idea that I should save every single book I had ever read. It seemed like a great idea at first as I proudly displayed on my shelves all the books—from authors like Jack Welch, Stephen Covey, and James Hunter—that had taught me to be a better leader. They sat alongside all sorts of books on other subjects I was interested in, which included parenting, sociology, and biographies of people I admired such as Steve Jobs, Ben Franklin, and John McCain. As I got older, however, my bookshelves started to become overfilled. My answer to this problem was to keep buying new shelves, that is until a few years ago when I took the job of president of Maaco. As my wife and I were in the process of packing up to move to Charlotte, North Carolina, where the company is based, I stood in front of those bookshelves thinking about what a nuisance it was going to be to box up and move all those heavy books. That was when I decided enough was enough. The next day I took every single one of those books and donated them to our local public library.

I still read books at a ferocious rate. I'm still curious and believe there is always more to learn. But now, every time I read a book, instead of keeping it for myself, I pass it on. I take it to the office to give to someone or bring it to one of the kiosks that someone decided to put up around my neighborhood where you can take a book or leave a book. The older I get and the more success I have, the more I understand the importance of spreading the word and giving back what you get. I believe giving away books does this in its own small way. I hope that writing this book has done the same.

I started out, in the introduction, by talking about the best advice I had ever gotten, which happened to be from my father. I would like to end here with a last word of advice about something I have learned along the way: *You have to take ownership.* You have to own your career, your values, your breadth of skills, your depth of knowledge. In short, you have to own everything about your life. No one is going to own these things for you.

For many of the young people I meet today, this often means taking ownership of the course of their careers. There have been many times when I have had someone come into my office demanding to know when he or she is going to get a raise or a promotion. My response to that person is always the same: "What have you done to earn that raise or promotion?" It's never really about what I can give these young people; it's about what they have done for themselves to get where they want to go.

Many of the established leaders I have known need to take ownership in a different area: over the balance in their lives. They are overworked, overstressed, and under-resourced, and it has taken a toll. This is a state of being that will lessen anyone's effectiveness, no matter how smart or accomplished they are. It makes people less effective as parents, as partners, as leaders, and simply as human beings interacting in the world. Yet I often hear people in the office say they can't possibly take time away from their work to spend time with their families, get to the gym, or whatever else they are itching to do. It never seems to occur to some of them that if they make time to do these things, it will have a positive impact on their work over the long term. As I've already alluded to in this book, everyone needs to take responsibility for figuring out what will sustain them as they find the courage and daily tenacity within themselves to pursue the lives they want. For me, I'm simply not able to achieve peak performance unless I have the following things in my life in balance: 1) faith, 2) family, 3) community, and 4) business.

Ultimately, each one of us is responsible for striking the right balance in our lives, for setting our own values and living by them each and every day. If you wait for someone else to set them for you, if you wait for conditions to be right, it may never happen.

By the same token, if you want to learn how to be a truly effective leader and to avoid the mistakes that leaders before you have made repeatedly — the kind of mistakes that lead to those dismal engagement numbers year after year that I talked about at the outset of this book — then you have to take responsibility for making the change. That's the only way to ensure that what I've talked about in this book doesn't just become another bit of wisdom sitting on the shelf. Instead, it can become an active part of your life, one that makes a real difference for you, your family, your community, your team members, your colleagues, and the organization in which you lead.

You have the power, the knowledge, and the tools you need to gain that leading edge. Now, let's see what you can do with them.

ABOUT THE AUTHOR

Jose R. Costa has a background steeped in marketing, franchising, multi-unit retailing and enhancing customer experience amongst some of the most recognized brands in the world. He currently serves as CEO of For Eyes, which is part of GrandVision, a global leader in optical retail with more than 7,000 stores worldwide, of which 120 are in the U.S.

Previous to his current role, he served as Group President of Driven Brands where he led MAACO®, CARSTAR® and Drive N Style®. Collectively, these brands operate more than 1,400 body shops across North America, generate more than $1.8 billion in annual system sales and further establish Driven Brands as a leader in the automotive aftermarket space. Previously, he was President of MAACO®, where he was responsible for managing and developing 500 automotive body shops across the U.S. and Canada. During his tenure, he improved MAACO®'s procedures and training practices, raised consistency among franchises, revamped operations and enhanced the look and feel of its advertising.

Before joining Driven Brands, Costa was Vice President of Marketing, R&D and Supply Chain at BURGER KING® where he grew Latin America's EBITDA from $50 million to $80 million in 26 months. Costa also served as President of COSTA IMC, a branding and interactive marketing firm focused on the U.S. Hispanic and Latin American segments.

Costa has over 20 years of experience both on the client and agency side, working for companies like Young & Rubicam, Bank of America, PepsiCo and YUM Brands. He also has extensive experience in restructuring portfolio companies for private equity firms like 3G Capital, Harvest Partners, Roark Capital and HAL Investments.

In 2017, Costa was a Gold Winner in the Executive of the Year category of the CEO World Awards. In 2016, he earned the Executive of the Year Gold Award in the Golden Bridge Awards®, an annual industry and peer recognition program honoring best companies in every major industry. He also won the Executive of the Year Bronze Stevie Award in the automotive and transport equipment industry in 2016. The Stevie Awards recognize outstanding performance in the workplace.

Costa was appointed to the Board of Trustees of Discovery Place for 2017-2020. He is also a National Association of Corporate Directors (NACD) Fellow, a credential that recognizes those committed to excellence in the boardroom, and a member of the Young Presidents Organization (YPO), the world's leading peer network of chief executives and business leaders.

In May 2018, Costa was inducted into Northwestern University's Medill Hall of Achievement, the highest honor of the School of Journalism, Media, and Integrated Marketing Communications. In April 2016, he was installed as the chapter leader of the Charlotte chapter of Chaîne des Rôtisseurs, the world's oldest and most prestigious food society. Costa also pursues social work with Big Brothers Big Sisters of Greater Miami, through which he has mentored a child in Miami for several years.

Costa has a postgraduate degree from Universidad Metropolitana, a Master's degree in Integrated Marketing Communications from Northwestern University and an MBA from the Booth School of Business at the University of Chicago.

Made in the USA
Columbia, SC
23 April 2021